TRAVEL

JAMAICA

By
CHRISTOPHER BAKER

Written by Christopher P Baker
Updated by Polly Rodger Brown

Original photography by Jon Wyand
Updated photography by Ethel Davies

Editing and page layout by Cambridge Publishing Management Ltd,
Unit 2, Burr Elm Court, Caldecote CB23 7NU
Series Editor: Karen Beaulah

Published by Thomas Cook Publishing
A division of Thomas Cook Tour Operations Ltd
Company Registration No. 1450464 England

PO Box 227, The Thomas Cook Business Park,
Coningsby Road, Peterborough PE3 8SB, United Kingdom
E-mail: books@thomascook.com
www.thomascookpublishing.com
Tel: +44 (0)1733 416477

ISBN: 978-1-84157-802-6

Text © 2007 Thomas Cook Publishing
Maps © 2007 Thomas Cook Publishing
First edition © 2005 Thomas Cook Publishing
Second edition © 2007 Thomas Cook Publishing

Project Editor: Diane Ashmore
Production/DTP Editor: Steven Collins

Printed and bound in Italy by: Printer Trento.

Front cover credits: Left © Natural Visions/Alamy; centre © Hans-Peter
Huber/SIME-4 Corners Images; right © Thomas Cook
Back cover credits: Left © Stuart Pearce/World Pictures; right © Bildagentur
Mauritius/World Pictures

Contents

KEY TO MAPS

■   Public building   𝑖 Information

▲
320m Mountain   ☀ Viewpoint

★   Start of walk   ✈ Airport

Introduction

Since Columbus chanced upon Jamaica 500 years ago, millions of visitors have discovered that it surely is 'the fairest island that eyes have beheld'. The Caribbean's third-largest island looks as if it were spawned from its own picture postcard. Here, Mother Nature has concentrated all the splendours she elsewhere sows parsimoniously throughout the tropics – cascading waterfalls, lush green mountains, ribbons of talcum-fine sand, the rustle of trade winds teasing the palms, flowers that spill their petals everywhere.

After a dark northern winter and the turmoils of a northern lifestyle, Jamaica soothes like a pleasant dream. You sense it the moment you arrive and are greeted by two of the very things you came to enjoy – fabulous sunny weather and the murmur of surf echoing across a sea as warm and as flat as a glass of milk at bedtime.

You can, if you wish, spend your days on the beach, being lulled to sleep by the whisper of waves, working up a healthy tan aided by the sun god himself. But that is just one of a choice

of plenty. You can also whisk across the bright turquoise shallows on a windsurfing board, sunfish sailing boat, or water-skis, or head out into the cobalt-blue sea to snorkel or dive. If a

Jamaica

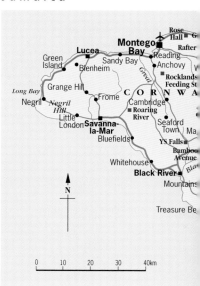

day out on a boat appeals, try your hand at deep-sea game fishing.

Away from the shore, Jamaica tickles every taste bud – there is so much to see and do it is difficult to know where to start. Should you take a romantic raft through green canyons, or maybe a horse ride in the cool Blue Mountains? Play golf, climb a waterfall, tour a haunted mansion, explore a once sinful pirate city, picnic on an old colonial sugar plantation, or visit a museum to learn about Jamaica's brutal slave-era history!

There is also the flip side. Much of Jamaica is still engaged in survival. Kingston, the capital city and a major cultural centre, is marred by ghettos where drug wars are fought. Poverty gnaws at the very edge of tourist resorts. This grande dame of the English-speaking Caribbean has weathered economic hard times in recent years – but the enchanting tropical beauty seems to wash away worries.

Jamaica's vibrant local culture is intense, complex and exciting. Reggae and Rastafarians, zesty cuisine and piquant patois are as much a part of the Jamaican experience as its natural beauty and fascinating history.

Add the widest selection of accommodation in the Caribbean – luxury hotels, thatched cottages by the sea, value-for-money villas and all-inclusive resorts – and you have the recipe for a holiday guaranteed to make you forget the worries of the world.

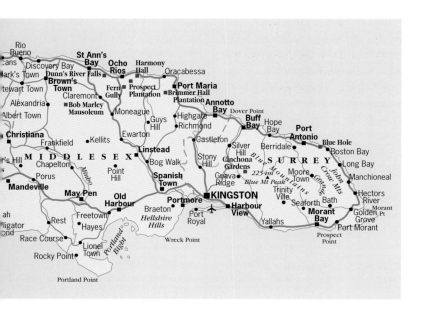

The land

Jamaica, which floats in the Caribbean sea 18° north of the equator, is 230km (146 miles) long, with widths varying between 35km (22 miles) and 81km (51 miles). It is roughly the size of Connecticut or half that of Wales. It has such acute variations in scenery, climate and character, however, that it is truly a world in one island.

Landscape

The name Jamaica derives from the Taino Indian word for their island, Xaymaca: 'land of wood and water'. And so it is, with countless rivers and waterfalls flowing down from mountains swathed in forests. The scalloped coastal plains and deeply incised central highlands are ripe with emerald meadows and fields of lime-green sugar cane, like sheets of green silk. The broad southern plain, however, in parts resembles the African savanna; it even has cactus and, in contrast, Everglades-like swamp. The beaches have their own contrasts – white sand in the west and north, black sand in the south.

Geology

Volcanic forces began to push the island up from the sea 30 million years ago – the limestone that covers two-thirds of Jamaica was once sea bed. A series of mountains forms the island's spine, soaring to 2,256m (7,402ft) at Blue Mountain Peak in the east, and almost half of Jamaica lies above 330m (1,000ft). The limestone plateaux – typified by the Cockpit Country – are pitted with depressions, sinkholes and caves.

Flora and fauna

This lush country is home to 3,000 species of plants (800 indigenous), including 200 orchid, 60 bromeliad and 550 fern species. In the Blue Mountains, bamboo, rhododendron and stunted dwarf forest are haunted by mists. Cacti rise from the parched earth of the south. Many of the fruit species were introduced; breadfruit was brought from the South Seas by Captain Bligh, the coconut came from Malaysia, ackee from Africa.

Mongooses were introduced to control rats, but they also decimated the native coney (a large guinea-piggish creature) and snakes (all harmless). Manatees survive along the south coast, alongside American crocodiles (confusingly called alligators in Jamaica). Jamaica's avifauna

The land

HURRICANES

In midsummer, northeast and southeast trade winds merge near the equator, spawning high-pressure squalls that centrifugal forces can whip into hurricanes. Jamaica has been hit by westward-moving hurricanes on several occasions. In recent memory Hurricane Ivan had the most disastrous effect when it struck in September 2004. The tropical cyclone lashed the country with 264kph (165mph) winds and torrential rains lasting over two days. Hurricane Ivan's effects were felt for months all over the island. The eastern and western areas were the most severely affected, especially Negril, where 20m (65ft) high tidal waves were recorded. Entire crops were lost. Much of Jamaica was without electricity. Roads, hospitals, schools and gardens were washed out and thousands of homes destroyed and people displaced.

includes hummingbirds, parrots and todies (*see pp84–5*).

Climate

Sun and trade winds bestow near-perfect weather. Temperatures seldom vary, averaging 28°C (82°F) year-round on the coast. The 'Doctor Breeze' helps keep you cool. The mountainous interior is crisper – cool and less humid. Midsummer (May–October) brings the bulk of the rain. Moisture-laden trade winds spill most of their rain on the mountains. The northeast is Jamaica's rainy corner. To the east of the mountains, the parish of Portland is Jamaica's rainiest place.

Population

Approximately 2.7 million people live on Jamaica, primarily of African origin, with minorities of European, East Indian and Chinese. Towns and cities contain 46 per cent of the population, with one-third of the island's population in Kingston.

Economy

Jamaica is a developing country. It faces a huge foreign debt, and though unemployment is officially quoted as 11.5 per cent, it's more likely to be as high as 35 per cent. Tourism is the leading industry and continues to grow. Bauxite, the mainstay of the economy in the 1960s and 1970s, today accounts for about 40 per cent of exports. The sugar-cane industry, once the country's biggest employer, is currently in crisis with huge debts, but products such as bananas, coffee and ackee continue to be exported.

This verdant scene is just one of the many varied landscapes of Jamaica

History

c. AD 650　The Taino Indians, originally from the Orinoco in Venezuela, reach Jamaica via the island of Hispaniola. They enslave the Saladoid Indians but gradually absorb the culture into their own.

1494　Columbus attempts to land at St Ann's Bay during his second voyage to the New World, but is driven off by the hostile Tainos. He lands next day at Discovery Bay. He names the island St Jago, or Santiago, after St James.

1503–4　Columbus returns during his fourth voyage, runs aground near St Ann's Bay, and is stranded for a full year.

1510　The Spaniards establish the colony of Sevilla Nueva and begin enslaving the Taino Indians. The Taino population of perhaps 100,000 is reduced within 150 years to less than 100.

1517　The first enslaved Africans arrive in Jamaica. For the next century the island remains little more than a supply base for Spain's other colonies.

1534　Sevilla Nueva is abandoned, and a new capital established at San Jago de la Vega (on the site of today's Spanish Town).

1655　A British fleet sails into Kingston harbour and captures Jamaica. The Spanish are allowed to escape to Cuba. They release their slaves, who flee to the hills and form the Maroons.

1658　The Spanish attempt to seize back Jamaica fails. They are defeated at the Battle of the Rio Nuevo.

Cannons at Fort Charles, Port Royal

The British colonise the island as part of Oliver Cromwell's Western Design – a grandiose scheme for expanding England's holdings in the Caribbean at the expense of Spain's.

1660s Governor Thomas Modyford gives buccaneers royal protection to harass Spanish colonies and ships. The buccaneers' base of Port Royal grows wealthy and earns the nickname 'the wickedest city in the world'.

1670 Jamaica is formally ceded to Britain by the Treaty of Madrid.

1690 Slaves rebel. The British respond brutally. Led by Cudjoe, Clarendon slaves ally with Maroons and launch the First Maroon War.

1692 An earthquake destroys Port Royal. The Jamaican government begins a crackdown on piracy and buccaneering.

1694 A French fleet under Admiral du Casse invades Jamaica and destroys over 50 sugar plantations, but is defeated at Carlisle Bay.

1739 Maroons sign treaty with British whereby they agree to capture runaway slaves and to assist in suppressing rebellions. In return they are given land and self-government.

1795 Second Maroon War breaks out. British troops import bloodhounds to hunt Maroons, who eventually sue for peace. More than 600 Maroons are deported to Canada, then to Sierra Leone, becoming the first Africans repatriated from the New World.

1807 Britain abolishes slave trade to British colonies.

1831 Black preacher 'Daddy' Sam Sharpe leads the Christmas slave rebellion around Montego Bay. Severe retribution by authorities fuels anti-slavery sentiment in England.

1834 British parliament passes Act abolishing slavery. In 1838 Britain pays compensation to Jamaican slaveholders and slavery finally ends in Jamaica. Indentured labourers imported from India.

1865	The Morant Bay Rebellion led by black deacon Paul Bogle is savagely repressed by the governor, who executes 430 'conspirators'. Parliament recalls the governor and makes Jamaica a British Crown Colony.
1872	The capital of Jamaica is moved from Spanish Town to Kingston.
1907	Much of Kingston is destroyed by a great earthquake. The new street plan is the basis for the city's layout today.
1938	Social disaffection fosters widespread violence and riots. Alexander Bustamante organises Jamaica's first officially recognised labour union. People's National Party (PNP) later founded by socialist Norman Manley.
1944	New constitution grants universal adult suffrage. Jamaica becomes fully self-governing, based on the British model of a bicameral parliament.
1962	Jamaica is granted independence, with Sir Alexander Bustamante as its first prime minister. The British monarch remains head of state, represented by a governor general. Jamaica enters the Commonwealth of Nations.
1972	PNP wins election. Michael Manley becomes prime minister, ushering in a period of leftist reform that generates economic instability. Subsequent elections are marred by violence.
1980	JLP (Jamaican Labour Party) wins election. Manley is succeeded by Edward Seaga, who returns Jamaica to a more moderate economic and political path. Hundreds of people are killed in election violence.
1988	Hurricane Gilbert devastates the island. Thousands of homes are destroyed.
1989	Manley is returned to power and takes a liberal conservative tack.
1992	Manley retires on health grounds. He is succeeded by Percival J Patterson.

1993	Led by Patterson, the PNP is returned to office with an increaseed majority.
1997	PNP retains power in landslide victory.
1999	People take to the streets in protest at a 30 per cent increase in fuel prices.
2002	PNP wins general elections for the fourth successive term. Patterson continues as prime minister. The World Bank approves a $129 million loan for financial-sector reform, secondary education and community-based infrastructure.
2004	After three decades in politics, Edward Seaga resigns as leader of the JLP. His successor is Bruce Golding.
2005	The new Caribbean Court of Justice is inaugurated in Trinidad. The intention to replace it with Britain's Privy Council in the Caribbean Commonwealth is a continuing debate since it will inevitably lead to the re-establishment of the death penalty in Jamaica, a popular move among islanders.
2006	Prime Minister P J Patterson resigns. Portia Simpson Miller becomes the country's first female prime minister and is hugely popular. In October, however, the opposition uncovers an undeclared J$31 million 'donation' to the PNP from Dutch oil trading company Trafigura. Simpson Miller's credibility is damaged but not irrevocably.

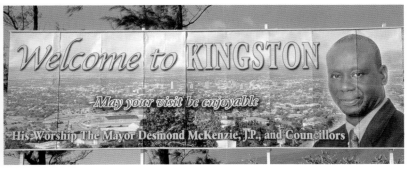

A welcoming sign at the outskirts of Kingston

Slavery

The Spaniards imposed their culture with the musket ball; the English imposed theirs with the chain and whip. Thus is Jamaica's history writ – painfully, as a slave colony.

From their earliest days the Spanish colonists enslaved the indigenous Taino population. Within a few decades the Indians were decimated and African slaves were imported to replace them.

The English who captured the island from Spain in 1655 swiftly developed Jamaica as a sugar economy, and huge fortunes were amassed by the cane planters (a new phrase came into British parlance: 'as wealthy as a West Indian planter'). The plantocracy established plantations throughout the island, and, to support the bustling estates, the British brought in thousands of African slaves. By the late 18th century, Jamaica had become a centre of the slave trade in the western hemisphere, with a population composed of about 300,000 black slaves and 20,000 whites.

Almost one in five Africans died during the Middle Passage – the horror-filled voyage across the Atlantic – when slaves were chained head-to-toe in the putrid bowels of slave ships. Less than

Ex-slave hospital, St Mary's Church, Shettlewood

RUN AWAY,

FROM

Orange River Plantation,

In the parish of St. Mary, in July 1778, a Creole NEGRO WOMAN named

MARY GOLD,

She was harboured some time past, at a Penn in Liguanea, but was seen about two months ago at Port-Henderson, big with child. Whoever harbours her, will be prosecuted according to law, but whoever apprehends her and will give information to WALTER POLLOCK, of said Plantation, or to THOMAS BELL in this town shall be handsomely rewarded.

Left, on said Plantation,

Silent reminders of the inhuman slave trade

half lived to be put to work in the fields.

The white plantocracy ran their estates through tyranny. Slaves were branded and commonly flayed, burned alive and otherwise brutally tortured.

The excesses were gradually controlled through Acts of Parliament, but the backbreaking field work and severity of life took its toll. Mortality was so great that six slaves died for each birth on the island. Over 600,000 slaves were imported to Jamaica between 1700 and 1807, when the trade was abolished. Yet the slave population was only 250,000 in 1834, the year of emancipation.

Not surprisingly, slave uprisings were common. The plantocracy lived in fear of their lives, and rebellions were put down with brutal severity. The success of the slave revolt in Haiti in 1798 inspired slave revolts throughout the Caribbean.

In December 1831, a Baptist preacher named Sam Sharpe led 20,000 slaves in gaining control of a plantation near Montego Bay. The English quashed the revolt by announcing that parliament had abolished slavery. In vengeful retribution, more than 1,000 slaves were executed. 'Daddy' Sharpe was hanged in the Montego Bay square that today bears his name.

It was the severity of this punishment that helped force the passage of the 1834 law abolishing slavery throughout the British Empire.

Politics

Jamaica borrows heavily from the British political stage in tradition and institution. The island is one of the Caribbean's oldest and most stable democracies. Nevertheless, it lends singular, often unbridled, partisan passions to the scene, and political violence at election time commonly makes worldwide news.

Constitution

Jamaica is an independent state and a member of the British Commonwealth of Nations. Under the 1962 Constitution, the Queen of England is head of state (the Queen of Jamaica), represented by a governor general whose functions are mostly ceremonial. The governor general is appointed on the recommendation of the Jamaican prime minister.

The island is also a parliamentary democracy. Political power is vested in parliament, a bicameral body consisting of the House of Representatives with 60 members and a Senate with 21 members. The representatives are elected by a simple majority in the constituencies they represent. The prime minister appoints 13 members of the Senate; the remainder are appointed by the leader of the opposition.

National elections are held every five years, and all nationals over 18 have the right to vote if they have registered. The leader of the political party that wins a simple majority becomes prime minister.

Local government

Jamaica is divided into 14 parishes, each run by an elected council. The parishes of Kingston and St Andrew together form the Kingston Metropolitan Area. The senior justice of the peace (judge) holds the ceremonial position of Custos Rotulorum, the queen's representative for each parish. The three counties (Cornwall, Middlesex and Surrey) no longer have a political function.

Political parties

Two major political parties dominate the scene and have alternated in power since the first national election in 1944.

The People's National Party (PNP) espouses 'democratic socialism'. It was formed in 1938 by barrister Norman Manley. Manley was succeeded as leader of the PNP in 1969 by his son Michael, a journalist and trade unionist who, as prime minister (1972–80), adopted a progressive yet controversial and eventually a destabilising leftist policy.

When re-elected in 1989, Manley went from anti-American firebrand to middle-of-the-road tourism promoter. He resigned due to ill health in 1992. The party was then led for 14 years by lawyer P J Patterson. He was the nation's first black prime minister and was succeeded on retirement in 2006 by Portia Simpson Miller, Jamaica's first female prime minister. Simpson Miller is a much-loved populist who is known for her folksy approach to politics.

The Jamaica Labour Party (JLP) was formed in 1943 by labour leader Alexander Bustamante (he and Norman Manley were cousins). Despite its name, the JLP is essentially a pro-business, conservative party.

The party was headed until recently by Edward Seaga, who as prime minister (1980–89) attempted to revive a collapsed economy. The PNP had boycotted the 1983 elections and Seaga basically ran a one-party state until 1989. His policies are generally accepted as having succeeded in rekindling the economy, despite worsening poverty for the majority of Jamaicans. The social distress cost him the 1989 election. In 2004, Seaga resigned after three decades in politics. The party is now led by Bruce Golding who is widely seen as ineffectual. The liberal United People's Party and the National Democratic Movement, a breakaway faction of the JLP, are the other main parties.

POLITICAL VIOLENCE

Patronage dominates Jamaican politics. In 1976, the political polarisation boiled over in the ghettos of Kingston, where militant party supporters enforced their political stranglehold through vigilantes. In 1980 the ghettos exploded. More than 700 died in battles between adherents of the PNP and JLP.

Since then, party leaders have sought to quell violence. In the 1989 and 1993 elections, 'only' 25 people lost their lives. Since then, there hasn't been a return to the 1980s' level of violence during elections, though tensions still run high in pre-election periods with the occasional shoot-out and an increased death rate, particularly in West Kingston.

All quiet now, but tempers can flare at election time in Jamaica

Rastafarians

No visitor to Jamaica can fail to notice the Rastafarians (Rastas) with their red, gold and green woollen tams and wildly tangled beards and hair. Jamaica's cultural rebels are often misunderstood. Despite their wild looks, Rastas live by a philosophy of peace and brotherly love.

Their prophet is Marcus Garvey (1887–1940), a Jamaican national hero and black rights advocate who, in 1919, predicted the crowning of a black king – the Redeemer – in Africa. In 1930 Ras Tafari Makonnen (*Ras*, an honorific given to royalty; *tafari*, the family name) was crowned Emperor Haile Selassie of Ethiopia. Biblical references to support

Haile Selassie, the Emperor of Ethiopia

Colourful hats

Selassie's divinity were touted, and a following emerged in Jamaica. Rastafarians consider Selassie to be a direct descendant of King Solomon and adopted Selassie's former name for themselves.

Rastas grow their hair without combing it until it twists and mats into locks – 'dreadlocks' – that may dangle below the waist. They are guided in this by the biblical passage, 'They shall not make baldness upon their head, neither shall they shave off the corner of their beard...' (Leviticus 21:5).

A Rasta's whole life is a non-violent protest against oppression. They believe themselves one of the lost tribes of Israel delivered into exile by the whites and left wandering in Babylon – Jamaica. Oppression is also 'Babylon', as are authority figures and institutions: the police, government, and so on. One day God – Jah – is expected to lead them back to Ethiopia, their Promised Land, or Zion.

Traditionalist Rastas prefer to live a simple life in the country, away from the pollution of Babylon. The most ardent are vegetarians with fastidious taboos. They eat only *I-tal* – natural foods. They are also teetotallers and non-smokers, despite their reverence for *ganja* (marijuana), which they consume copiously. Smoking *ganja* – 'wisdom weed' or the 'sacred herb' – is considered a religious act, often accompanied by recitations of prayers and psalms. A *ganja* pipe is known as a chalice, and is ideally made of cow or goat horn (but more usually wood).

Rastas take great pride in black history and artistic and athletic attainment while honouring codes against avarice, dishonesty, exploitation and sexual envy. They eschew the Christian concept of redemption in favour of the concept of heaven in the here and now.

Jamaica's politicians often pay homage to Rastafarianism in recognition of its sway. The creed has also lent many colourful phrases to the Jamaican dialect: 'one love', a parting expression meaning peace or unity, for example, and 'cool runnings', a goodbye, blessing and encouragement.

Rasta dreadlocks

Culture

Jamaica's proud motto is 'out of many, one people'. The island is a spectrum of races: decades of intermarriage have produced features and shades of every colour.

There's always time for the donkey to have a quick snack

The vast majority of Jamaicans – 95 per cent – are descendants of African slaves or their unions with European masters. (Black Jamaicans regard themselves as Jamaicans and like to be referred to as such, not as 'natives' – a term that historically was used to connote uncivilised or primitive.) Significant minorities whose ancestors came from Lebanon, Germany, India and China stitched their identities on to the soul and sinew of Jamaican culture.

The island's savage history has imbued Jamaicans with a fierce independence and pride – traits they share with Anancy, a spider and folk hero who grapples with a harsh world by deviousness, a sharp intelligence and quick wit. Jamaicans are opinionated and often argumentative, but politeness and courtesy are also part of the national heritage. Jamaicans are quick to give and respond to a hearty 'Good morning!' Above all, they are friendly – and funny. Their

REGGAE

It's almost impossible to imagine Jamaica without its distinctive music of reggae. First used as a medium for political commentary, the name sprang from Toots and the Maytals' 1968 hit *Do the Reggay*. The 1972 film, *The Harder They Come*, brought reggae's rhythms and celebrities to a wider audience. Musicians such as Peter Tosh and Jimmy Cliff have been exponents of the style, with Bob Marley remaining the iconic legend of the genre. The sounds are vibrant and current, yet continue to inspire offshoots, such as Dancehall, one of the latest musical movements.

deprecating sense of humour is subtle, sardonic and often bawdy.

The average Jamaican dresses conservatively, but in other regards he or she is permissive. Casual sexual liaisons, for example, are common. Jamaican women are proudly independent and may typically have children by several men before marrying relatively late in life. Nevertheless, beside the beds of many Jamaicans lies the King James Version of the Bible. (The island has more churches per mile than any other country in the world!) The Anglican Church has the largest membership. Rastafarianism is another potent force (*see pp16–17*), and ancient African spiritual practices, revived after the abolition of slavery (*pukkamina*, *kumina* and *obeah*), linger on.

The African heritage is deeply rooted in Jamaican song and dance. The rhythm of reggae, the heartbeat of the nation, owes much to the beat of the African drum. You will hear it all over the island, an elemental expression of joy in the face of hardship.

A lazy day with the white sand and green waters of the Caribbean

Festivals and events

January

Accompong Maroon Festival
Annual celebration of Maroon culture with traditional singing, dancing, feasting and ceremonies. Accompong, St Elizabeth. *Tel: (876) 971 3900; www.visitjamaica.com*

Air Jamaica Jazz and Blues Festival
Annual music event attracting well-known singers of the genre.
Tel: (876) 754 1526; www.visitjamaica.com

February

Pineapple Cup Yacht Race
Annual 1,305km (811-mile) race from Miami to Montego Bay.
Montego Bay Yacht Club. *Tel: (876) 979 8038; www.montegobayrace.com*

Bob Marley Birthday Bash
Annual celebration, islandwide, of Marley's birthday on 6 February, with big-name concerts and sound-system jams.
Tel: (876) 927 9152; www.bobmarley-foundation.com

A Fi Wi Sinting
Celebration of Jamaica's African heritage, with food and clothes stalls, poetry recitals and live music. Buff Bay, Portland. *Tel: (876) 715 3529; www.fiwisinting.com*

March

Spring Break
A month of live music and booze-fuelled beach parties. Montego Bay and Negril.

Tel: (876) 952 4425; www.visitjamaica.com

St Ann's Kite Festival and Family Fun Day
Home-made kites of all shapes and sizes, with a fun-fair and games for children. Seville Great House, St Ann's Bay.
Tel: (876) 972 2191; www.jnht.com

April

Trelawney Yam Festival
Four days of yam-filled fun. Hague Show Grounds, Trelawney.
Tel: (876) 610 0818; www.stea.net

Carnival
A month-long party which finally ends with a parade through Kingston and the crowning of the Carnival King and Queen. Kingston and islandwide.
Tel: (876) 923 9138; www.jamaicacarnival.com

Jamaica Polo Association Tournament and Horse Show
Combined event with top polo from around the world. St Ann's Polo Club, St Ann's Bay. *Tel: (876) 383 5586.*

May

Calabash Literary Festival
A multi-day festival celebrating some of the best Caribbean literature around, complete with guest speakers and participants. Treasure Beach, South Coast. *Tel: (876) 965 3000; www.calabashliteraryfestival.org*

June
Ocho Rios Jazz Festival
Annual, week-long series of concerts by local as well as international jazz musicians. Ocho Rios. *Tel: (876) 927 3544; www.ochoriosjazz.com*

July
Reggae Sumfest
Reggae's biggest celebration, featuring world-class stars. Catherine Hall, Montego Bay. *Tel: (876) 953 2933; www.reggaesumfest.com*
Portland Jerk Festival
Annual celebration of one of Jamaica's finest foodstuffs, jerked pork. Boston Bay, Portland. *Tel: (876) 993 3051; www.visitjamaica.com*

August
Independence Day Celebrations
Traditional Jonkanoo dancers and modern dancers showcase a cross-section of Jamaican culture. Islandwide events, including a gala street parade in Kingston. *Tel: (876) 926 5726; www.jcdc.org.jm*
Jamerican Film Festival
Festival celebrating Jamaican and Caribbean films and film-makers. Live music events also. Montego Bay. *Tel: (001) 323 936 8951; www.jamericanfilmfestival.com*

September
Montego Bay International Marlin Competition
An annual game-fishing tournament, begun in 1967 and still going strong.

Montego Bay Yacht Club. *Tel: (001) 323 936 8951; www.montego-bay-jamaica.com*

October
Port Antonio International Marlin Competition
One of the oldest and most prestigious game-fishing tournaments in the Caribbean. Port Antonio Marina. *Tel: 876 927 0145; www.errolflynnmarina.com*
Old Harbour Fish and Bammy Festival
Annual culinary festival and family day out with fish recipes, tasting and story-telling for children. Kingston. *Tel: (876) 359 5972; www.visitjamaica.com*

November
Kingston Restaurant Week
Annual event which gives diners the opportunity to taste gourmet food at some of Kingston's finest restaurants for a fraction of the regular cost. Kingston. *Tel: (876) 978 6245; www.visitjamaica.com*

December
Reggae Marathon
Coastal run accompanied by pounding reggae music. Negril. *Tel: (876) 922 8677; www.reggaemarathon.com*
National Art Biennial
Biennial event which features the work of Jamaica's best artists, both living on the island and abroad. National Gallery, Kingston. *Tel: (876) 922 1561; www.galleryjamaica.com*

Impressions

Jamaica is all you expect. Glorious weather... superb beaches... reggae and rum... and scenic beauty that is unsurpassed. But then again, it is not what you expect. Misconceptions about Jamaica are rife. A little advance knowledge will better acquaint you.

Crime

Jamaica has a worldwide reputation for violent crime, spawned by political violence (mostly in Kingston) during the late 1970s. The negative publicity, however, has left an indelible image. Actually, Jamaica is much safer than many people think, but it must be recognised that opportunistic theft does occur. In 1994, the Jamaican government introduced a sweeping anti-crime initiative in major resort towns, and this legislation has had a positive effect (*see also p182*).

Take the same precautions you would in any unfamiliar destination. Always leave any valuables in your hotel safe, and do not wear jewellery. Carry no more money than you need, use money belts and keep wallets out of view. Avoid walking in poorly lit streets or on remote beaches at night. In addition, avoid Kingston's ghettos, where gun battles are fought over drug wars and politics, and violence is rife.

Driving

Main highways are generally well paved. However, the road that skirts the east coast and secondary roads that wind inland can be rough. A major building initiative is rapidly improving driving surfaces. High in the mountains, roads are often reduced to what amounts to a set of stairs that your car ascends with difficulty.

Rural Jamaicans refer to precipitous paths hacked out of the steep hillside as 'roads'. Roads that are passable for vehicles are called 'drivin' roads'.

Jamaicans drive on the left. Remember the local saying: 'The left side is the right side. The right side is suicide!'

Jamaicans are fast drivers. They like to overtake and are often reckless in doing so. Jamaican drivers are not particularly courteous (they're often argumentative and will even stop to hurl abuse at drivers who cross them). They often creep through red lights or disregard them altogether, so be particularly careful at junctions.

Watch for people, as well as goats and chickens, wandering on the road. Pay particular attention when driving at night; brown cattle often stray in front of vehicles and are impossible to see in the dark. Additionally, Jamaicans rarely dip their headlights.

Finding your feet

Jamaica's poverty can come as a shock. Steel yourself! Also, prepare yourself for a much slower pace of life. Patience and good humour are required in restaurants and elsewhere. And adopt Jamaican time – slow!

Do not be surprised, too, if you're called by such names as 'whitey' (if you're black you're most likely to be treated to the 'Hey bredrin' (brother) or 'sister' approach). It is not derogatory.

Such blunt terms are used merely as tags of identification. And do not take undue offence at what may appear to be arrogance; Jamaicans are often argumentative and opinionated without intended malice.

Ganja (marijuana)

The chances are that you will not be in Jamaica long before someone offers you *ganja* – marijuana. The 'sacred herb' was introduced in the 19th century by indentured labourers from India and has since become an integral part of Jamaican culture. To Rastafarians it is sacred – the staff of life.

Many Jamaicans depend on marijuana – 'the poor man's friend' – for their income (St Ann, the 'Garden Parish', is commonly called the '*Ganja*

You will see a police presence on the streets

Parish'). It generates hundreds of millions of dollars a year in foreign exchange from illegal sales.

Beachside hagglers, known locally as 'higglers', are likely to try to sell you some 'smoke' – regardless of your age or appearance.

The possession and sale of drugs is strictly illegal, and offenders face strict punishment. Random road searches are common, and tourists are favourite targets.

Getting around

The domestic airline Air Jamaica (*www.airjamaica.com*) runs a frequent shuttle service between Montego Bay and Kingston. Charter air service International Air Link (*www.intlairlink.com*) operates regular flights to Negril and Ocho Rios and can also be chartered to Port Antonio.

The bus system is a cheap option, but not recommended unless you are looking for adventure! Although a great way to meet the locals, it is very disorganised, overcrowded, and operates to no set timetable. Car-hire charges can give you a shock, but there are plenty of rental companies to choose from (*see pp183–4*). Hiring a reputable taxi driver for the day is a common practice. Though relatively expensive, it's a great way to see the island.

Haggling

Bargaining – 'haggling' or 'higgling' – is a way of life. Prices in markets and from beach or roadside vendors are always negotiable. Regard shopping as a sport and you will have fun. Getting real bargains will thoroughly test your skills!

A stall selling straw hats and baskets

Hustlers

Jamaicans in popular tourist areas can be aggressive in their sales pitch. You may be pressured to buy unwanted items and to pay for unwanted services, real or imagined, and offers commonly include prostitution – by both men and women. If long-haired, you will be cajoled to have your hair braided. Or you may be asked to pay for a photograph innocently taken: 'Jus' give sometin' for I, jus' a likkle.'

Say 'No!' – firmly, but in a friendly tone – then expect to say it again. The persistence can chafe, though it is not threatening. Beneath the pushiness is usually a warmth that can be drawn out by a smile.

Not many customers just now at this shop in Hagley Gap

Lie of the land

Montego Bay, on the northwest coast, is Jamaica's most convenient and popular resort, with fine beaches, an active nightlife and a bustling city centre.

Ocho Rios, a beautiful 90-minute drive east from Mo'Bay, follows a slower pace and is a magnet for a panoply of sightseeing excursions. This popular tourist resort is favoured by cruise ships.

Port Antonio lies way to the east – a magnificent and occasionally white-knuckle drive over the Blue Mountains or around the south coast from Kingston. Slightly down-at-heel but with reclusive, up-market resorts nestled in secluded coves.

Negril, Jamaica's westernmost outpost and self-proclaimed party town, is a 90-minute drive from Mo'Bay. It blends a stunning beach and fabulous water sports with a laid-back, anything-goes lifestyle.

Mandeville lies far from the madding crowds in the mountainous heart of Jamaica, a two-hour drive south from Mo'Bay or Ocho Rios. The untramelled south coast lies within easy reach.

Patois

'Walk good' is not a grammatical error. It is a Jamaican saying, and means 'safe journey'. The Queen's English is the official language, but Jamaica's unofficial lingo is the local patois – a linguistic frontier almost impenetrable to the visitor.

You'll see a lot of smiling, happy faces in Jamaica

'Jamaican talk' twists the mother tongue, adds slang, and peppers it with Spanish, African, Irish, Welsh and other words that have all found their way into the broth.

The result is often lewd and laconic. For 'Mind your own business', there is 'Cockroach no bizness in a fowl-yard'; for the pretentious, there is 'Monkey, the higher 'im climb, the more 'im expose'. Instead of 'I love you', a Jamaican paramour may say, 'Girl, me luv you to det', free food and money forget.'

'Cool runnings' is patois for 'good-bye' and also a blessing. Two phrases you will hear often are 'Irie' and 'No problem'. They mean everything is fine. Relax. Be cool!

Stay for just a few days and you will be talking Jamaican, too.

Nude bathing

Though Jamaica is a sexually permissive society, it is also old-fashioned and very religious. Nude or topless sunbathing is rare among Jamaicans and not tolerated on public beaches. Many all-inclusive hotels have roped-off nude bathing areas, particularly those catering to couples only (Sandals and Couples) and the Hedonism resorts. Negril is known for its 'anything goes' culture and topless bathing is acceptable on its Long Bay beach.

The other Jamaica

Tourism has not completely taken over Jamaica – the island still holds the promise of mystery. It has beaches, but it also has bush. Away from the beach resorts an entirely different experience lies close at hand, yet a world away, along roads that are portals to vibrant market towns and off-the-beaten-track villages (though you should take advice before venturing too far on your own – some areas are not recommended). Here you can experience traditional life and discover that, despite Jamaica's lingering poverty, her smile is full-blossomed and bright. If going independently is too much of a challenge, there are several tour companies offering alternative tours (*see Directory, Organised tours, p186*).

When to go

Jamaica has a balmy year-round climate. On the coast, temperatures are always warm and vary only slightly (*see p7*) with the seasons. The cooler, drier months are December to April; most salubrious of all is February and March.

Impressions

You will pay more for the pleasure – hotels charge higher prices during peak season.

If you do not mind extra rain, visit in May to October. September and October, the rainiest months, are a good time to visit the drier south coast.

Hotels and tour operators slash their rates from mid-April to mid-December, when a less hurried pace prevails. Mid-summer may be busier, when locals take their holiday.

What to wear

Pack light, loose-fitting cotton garments. A sweater or light jacket is needed for the highlands and even some nights on the coast. What you wear to dinner will depend on where you are dining. Many up-market resorts and restaurants require jackets and ties for men, and dresses for ladies. Elsewhere, Jamaican formality merely means putting on shoes. Dress code for

MEET THE PEOPLE

The ideal way to learn about Jamaica is in the company of a Jamaican friend. The Jamaican Tourist Board's Meet the People programme will match you up with a local person or family for an afternoon at the beach, a religious service, a picnic in the mountains or a night of reggae. The governor and his wife might even invite you for tea! Almost 1,000 families are registered hosts. You spend as much time with your new Jamaican friends as you like. The programme is free, and all expenses incurred are borne by the host (show your appreciation with a gift).
Tel: (876) 929 9200; www.visitjamaica.com; in the UK: tel: (0207) 225 9090; in the USA: tel: (305) 665 0557.

discos is simple – just throw on a T-shirt to 'ride de reggae riddims'.

If you burn easily, pack long-sleeved shirts and full-length dresses, plus sunhats. Tropical downpours can be sudden and heavy, and an umbrella is more practical than a raincoat.

Bamboo Avenue, a two-mile glade of giant bamboos

Kingston

Contrary to popular opinion, Kingston is not all, or even mostly, a ghetto. The metropolis – the largest English-speaking city south of Miami – is the intellectual centre of Jamaica, as well as the cultural capital of the Caribbean. The richly layered city resonates with music, theatre and dance. Kingston is also a perfect base for exploring the historic pirate haunt of Port Royal and the enchanting Blue Mountains.

Kingston, the nation's capital (population 800,000), is not a beautiful city, though its waterfront setting against the soaring Blue Mountains is dramatic. Its outskirts are surrounded by industry – bauxite, cement, oil, flour – and shacks no bigger than a one-car garage nailed together with planks and strips of tin. The bustle of energy grows as you close in on the city centre.

Downtown, near the wharves of the world's seventh-largest natural harbour, is the oldest part of the city. Much of the decent colonial architecture is here, including theatres that are venues for the Jamaica Philharmonic, the National Chorale, the Jamaican Folk Singers and the widely acclaimed National Dance Theatre Company.

New Kingston, to the north, is a more relaxed region of high-rise offices, banks, insurance companies, and parks. It is anchored by Half Way Tree, a square where old and new Kingston meet. Hope Gardens, the island's foremost botanic gardens, is here. So

too are Devon House, Kings House (home to the governor general), Jamaica House (the prime minister's office), the University of the West Indies, and a range of restaurants reflecting the world's best cuisines.

On the city outskirts are Caymanas Park (a venue for horse racing) and two 18-hole championship golf courses. Less than an hour away you can be high up in the mountains, sampling coffee and the magnificent view… or exploring the remains of Port Royal, erstwhile pirate capital of the Caribbean, half an hour's drive away across the harbour. Near Port Royal are the Cays, uninhabited white-sand islands good for snorkelling and bathing.

Day and night, Kingston vibrates with reggae, the cool-hot musical phenomenon that was born in the ghettos and is sure to put a spring in your step (for an appreciation of reggae, visit the Bob Marley Museum, *see opposite*). Avoid the ghettos, such as Trench Town, Jongs Town and Tivoli

Gardens, which stretch for miles. Here 'rude boys' or gang leaders rule their territories with guns. Outsiders cannot enter without permission. Nor would you want to! Thirty years ago Kingston was a mecca for tourists. There are long-standing plans to gentrify the downtown area, and the city authorities are working hard to convince today's travellers that it is a fascinating – and safe – place to visit.

Bob Marley Museum

The late Bob Marley's home and Tuff Gong recording studio is now a museum – the most visited site in Kingston – that chronicles his life from ghetto to reggae superstardom and premature death. A statue of Marley holding his guitar stands in front of the porticoed entrance.

Hour-long tours lead you through the grounds and modestly decorated house containing Marley's gold and platinum records, Rastafarian religious cloaks and other memorabilia. The old recording studio is now an exhibition hall and theatre.

Outside, your guide will point out the tall shade tree beneath which Marley smoked *ganja* (marijuana), as well as bullet holes in the rear of the house from an assassination attempt in 1976.

56 Hope Rd, Kingston 6. Tel: (876) 927 9152; www.bobmarley-foundation.com. Open: Mon–Sat 9.30am–5pm. Admission charge.

Coin and Notes Museum

The history of Jamaican tokens, coins and paper money is told in this tiny museum. Guided tours are offered.
Bank of Jamaica Building, Ocean Blvd, Kingston 1. Tel: (876) 922 0750; www.boj.org.jm. Open: Mon–Fri 9am–4pm.

THE JAMAICA TOURIST BOARD

64 Knutsford Boulevard, Kingston 5.
Tel: (876) 929 9200; www.visitjamaica.com

A splendid sunset gives way to the lights of Kingston at dusk

MA
BRO
COR

DUHANEY
PARK

PEMBROKE
HALL

CAMPER

A1

SIX
MILE

WASHINGTON   BOULEVARD   A1

Sandy Gu

Fresh

WASHINGTON
GARDENS

Spanish
Town

OLYMPIC
GARDENS

EAST
P

HA

St And
Ch

SPANISH TOWN ROAD

COCKBURN
GARDENS

RICHMONI
PARK

Cobre

A1

HAGLEY PARK ROAD

GREGORY
PARK

THREE
MILE

WATERFORD ROAD

WHITFIELD
TOWN

Caymanas
Park

SPANISH TOWN

PORTMORE-KINGSTON CAUSEWAY

*Hunts
Bay*

Tuff Gong
Studio

MARCUS GARVEY DRIVE

GREENWICH
TOWN

Naggo Head Spring

INDEPENDENCE
CITY

PASSAGE
FORT

PORTMORE PARKWAY

DAWKINS DRIVE

Gordon Cay

PORTMORE

NAGGO
HEAD

Fort Augusta

K i n g s

EDGEWATER

BRIDGEPORT

BRAETON

Port Henderson

Gallows
Point

Refuge
Cay

*Port Royal
Harbour*

Old Naval
Hospital

PORT
ROYAL

St Peter's
Church

Fort Charles

Giddy House

T h e   P a l i s a

Port
Royal
Point

*Green
Bay*

*Great
Salt
Pond*

Fort Clarence

Lime Cay

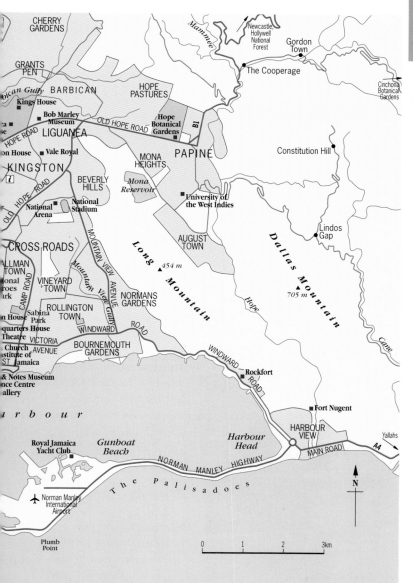

Devon House

This stately Georgian mansion was built in 1881 as the residence of George Stiebel, the first black Jamaican millionaire. The handsome structure was constructed entirely by Jamaicans and is set in shady grounds.

The government rescued Devon House from decay in the 1960s to house Jamaica's National Gallery, which has since moved to a new location. The house was restored and reopened for a visit by Queen Elizabeth II in January 1983. It is now a museum.

The interior is furnished in 1860s European-colonial style with bewitching hints of the tropics. The entrance hall, for example, has walls decorated with painted palm trees swaying in the breeze. An erstwhile gambling room is discreetly tucked away in the attic. The former stables now house an array of boutiques, craft

The palm trees in front of Devon House are matched by painted ones in the hall

stores and shops selling things ranging from essential oils and T-shirts to fabled Blue Mountain coffee. There is also an elegant restaurant, Norma's on the Terrace, a more informal place for casual lunches, the Grog Shoppe and a bakery, the Brick Oven, which sells famously good Jamaican patties.
26 Hope Rd, Kingston 10. Tel: (876) 929 6602; www.devonhousejamaica.com. Open: Mon–Sat 9.30am–5pm. Admission charge.

Gordon House

Gordon House was built in 1960 to seat Jamaica's House of Representatives. Within (and in its ceremony) it closely resembles the British House of Commons.

The House was named to honour the national hero and martyr George William Gordon, a coloured legislator, lay preacher and champion of the poor, who was hanged by a kangaroo court in reprisal for the Morant Bay Rebellion in 1865. The house of representatives meets here most afternoons at 2pm and visitors may watch proceedings, by prior arrangement, from the public gallery.
Corner of Beeston and Duke Sts. Tel: (876) 922 1287; www.jnht.com

Headquarters House

Parliament formerly sat in this elegant brick-and-plaster town house, built in 1750 by wealthy planter Thomas Hibbert in a wager with three other merchants as to who could build the finest house in order to secure the attentions of a beautiful lady.

Today it is the headquarters of the Jamaica National Heritage Trust.

The house is filled with antiques and fine art. Climb the lookout tower for a view over Kingston.

79 Duke St, Kingston 1. Tel: (876) 922 1287; www.jnhet.com. Open: Mon–Fri 8.30am–4.30pm. Admission free.

Half Way Tree

This chaotic crossroads at the junction of Hope Road and Constant Spring Road was once the old village centre of St Andrew's Parish. A large clock tower (erected in 1913 as a memorial to King Edward VII) occupies the centre.

Constant Spring Road leads north, flanked by aqueducts built in the 1770s on the estate that once stood here.

St Andrew's Parish Church

This church dates back to 1692, and was radically altered in the 1870s. Step inside to admire the organ and stained glass.

Hope Botanical Gardens

These public gardens, the largest botanical gardens in the Caribbean, occupy the old Hope Estate established by Major Richard Hope, who came to Jamaica with Cromwell's army in 1655. The gardens were established by the government in 1881 and today cover some 80 hectares (200 acres) below the Blue Mountains. Pathways lead past a lake, cactus garden, ornamental ponds,

greenhouses, flowering trees and shrubs. There is also an aquarium, a small, rather neglected zoo and a children's amusement park. The gardens are being restored after years of neglect.

Old Hope Rd, Kingston 10.
Tel: (876) 927 1257.
Gardens open: daily, 6am–6pm.
Zoo open: daily, 10am–5pm. Admission charge to zoo. Orchid house open:
Sat 9am–5pm. Admission charge.

Institute of Jamaica

The Institute was founded in 1879 for 'the encouragement of literature, science and art'. This headquarters houses the national archives, including the National Library (formerly the West Indian Reference Library, founded in 1894). The astonishing collection of documents recording the island's history and that of the Caribbean is the largest assemblage of West Indian material in the world.

The Institute's Natural History Division is also located here, and features a herbarium among its attractions. The building has rooms and a lecture hall, plus permanent and visiting exhibitions.

10–16 East St, Kingston 1. Tel: (876) 922 0620. National Library, tel: (876) 967 1526; www.instituteofjamaica.com.
National Library. Open: Mon–Thur 9am–5pm, Fri 9am–4pm.National History Division. Open: Mon–Thur 9.30am–4.30pm, Fri 9.30am–3.30pm.
Admission charge.

Jamaica House

This modern building was built in the 1960s as the residence of the prime minister. Today, it is used solely as his executive office. It stands behind sentried gates, amid expansive lawns with a driveway lined with lilies, gladioli and palms. Note the faded Picasso-style mural in the corner of the grounds as you walk up Hope Road.
Hope Rd, Kingston 6. Not open to the public.

Kings House

This building, by noted architect Sir Charles Nicholson, is the official residence of the governor general, the Queen's representative on the island. The house replaced an earlier structure, Bishop's Lodge, that was destroyed in the 1907 earthquake. Inside are several valuable paintings, including full-length portraits of King George III and Queen Charlotte by Sir Joshua Reynolds. It is surrounded by 80 hectares (200 acres) of well-tended lawns and parkland.

In front of the house is a giant banyan tree occupied, according to local legend, by *duppies* (ghosts).

The governor's wife often invites tourists to tea as part of the Jamaica Tourist Board's 'Meet the People' programme (*see p27*).
Hope Rd, at the corner of East Kings House Rd. Tel: (876) 927 6424. Open: Mon–Sat 9am–5pm by appointment; contact Jamaica Tourist Board for opening details. Free admission.

National Gallery

Opened in 1984, the National Gallery houses an impressive collection of contemporary and historical works by Jamaica's most exciting artists. The permanent collections include noteworthy sculptures by Edna Manley, the talented wife of the nation's second prime minister, plus almost 100 hardwood sculptures by famed local artist Kapo.

A biennial national exhibition is mounted every December (*see p21*).
Roy West Building, 12 Ocean Blvd. Tel: (876) 922 1561; www.galleryjamaica.com. Open: Tue–Thur 10am–4.30pm, Fri & Sat 10am–4pm. Admission charge.

National Heroes Park

This former racecourse in the heart of downtown Kingston is now a 30-hectare (75-acre) park containing memorials to Jamaica's national heroes: Paul Bogle, George William Gordon, Sam Sharpe and Maroon chief Nanny, Marcus Mosiah Garvey, founder of the Universal Negro Improvement Association. Former prime minister Sir Donald Sangster is buried here, as are politicians Norman Manley and Alexander Bustamante. Also here are Simon Bolivar, the South American liberator, and General Antoneo Maceo, a Cuban nationalist hero. The Jamaica War Memorial honours the nation's fallen.
North end of Duke St, 1km (½ mile) north of The Parade. Free admission.

The Parade

The Parade, in the bustling centre of town, is the chaotic terminus for Kingston's bus system. It was once a military parade ground with a public gallows and stocks. At its heart is **Sir William Grant Park**, shaded by trees laid out in 1870. It has a fountain as well as several statues of various illustrious Jamaicans. A statue of Queen Victoria faces King Street.

The park is named after a labour leader of the 1930s, who used the steps of Coke Chapel (on the eastern side of The Parade) as his oratory platform. The chapel, the cradle of Methodism in Jamaica, dates from 1790.

Ward Theatre

The ornate Ward Theatre, on the north side of The Parade, was built in 1907 on the site of the municipal Theatre Royal and presented to the city in 1911 by Colonel Charles Ward, Custos of Kingston (*see p14*). Jamaica's vibrant theatrical traditions still thrive within.

The Ward hosts performances by the National Dance Theatre Company and amateur drama groups, as well as the annual pantomime, which opens on Boxing Day (26 December) and usually runs through to April. The patois is often dense, but the spontaneous audience reactions and vivid slapstick style make a visit worthwhile.
North Parade, Kingston 1.
Tel: (876) 922 0453.

The elegant Ward Theatre in Kingston

University of the West Indies

The attractive 256-hectare (635-acre) campus of the University of the West Indies is wedged between the Hope River and the Long Mountains. The main attraction is the simple, cut-stone chapel near the main entrance. The chapel was transported stone by stone from the Gale Valley Estate in Trelawny.

The university was built in 1948 on the ruins of the old Mona sugar estate. Portions of the aqueduct and factory buildings can still be seen.

Stunning murals depicting island life grace the outside walls of the Assembly Hall and Caribbean Mass Communication Building.
Off Mona Rd, in the Papine area of Kingston.

Vale Royal

The official residence of the prime minister is a beautifully restored, gleaming white, colonnaded colonial structure topped by a dovecote-style lookout tower. The old house has been in continuous use since 1694. It was built by a wealthy planter.
Montrose Rd off Lady Musgrave Rd.
Not open to the public.

Walk: Kingston

Far from the ghettos of downtown Kingston, Uptown (New Kingston) is a relatively prosperous and peaceful residential and business section. A walk through this area will reveal several appealing features, including some architectural gems and a landmark museum. Strollers feel Kingston's adrenalin-charged edge, but are spared the entreaties of hustlers. Most tourist hotels are a few minutes walk or drive from the starting point.

Allow 2 hours, excluding museum visit.

Start at the Jamaica Tourist Board headquarters on Knutsford Blvd. Walk three blocks to Trafalgar Rd. Turn left and continue past the venerable Courtleigh Hotel (on your left) to Hope Rd. The grounds of Devon House

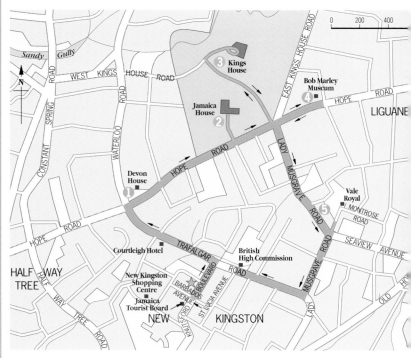

command the northeast corner (note the intriguing, down-at-heel colonial-era structure on the southwest corner, now the YMCA).

1 Devon House

This elegant mansion, built in 1881, is superbly furnished with period antiques. Behind the house is a fascinating array of boutiques, craft shops and stores selling everything from ice cream to essential oils. The Grog Shoppe and Norma's on the Terrace restaurants are in the former stables and carriage house, where you can dine alfresco in the airy courtyard beneath a massive mahogany tree (*see also p32*).
Continue up Hope Rd to Jamaica House.

2 Jamaica House

The former residence of the prime minister (now his office), with a white-columned portico facing the road, was built in the 1960s. It is fronted by pleasing lawns (*see also p34*).
Continue along Hope Rd to East Kings House Rd.

3 Kings House

The official residence of the governor general is set in 80 hectares (200 acres) of landscaped grounds. The governor's wife hosts 'Meet the People' tea parties. Enquire at the Jamaica Tourist Board (*see also p34*).
Continue up Hope Rd to the Bob Marley Museum.

4 Bob Marley Museum

The reggae legend's former home and recording studio has been turned into a museum-cum-shrine. The guided one-hour tour offers a fascinating insight into the life of the musical prodigy. In the grounds is the Queen of Sheba restaurant, which serves juices and I-tal vegetarian dishes (*see also p29*).
Return to East Kings House Rd. Turn left on to Lady Musgrave Rd. Walk south to the junction with Montrose Rd and Seaview Ave. Turn left. Vale Royal faces you on a right-angle bend.

5 Vale Royal

Vale Royal is the residence of the prime minister. The gleaming, two-storey wooden structure was built in 1694 by a wealthy planter, Simon Taylor, and later served as the home of the British Colonial Secretary (*see also p35*).
Finish at the British High Commission which is situated at the junction of Trafalgar Rd and St Lucia Rd.

Mural at the Tuff Gong recording studio, now part of the Bob Marley Museum

AROUND KINGSTON
Blue Mountains

The majestic Blue Mountains that rise northeast of Kingston are stupendously scenic and easily accessible. These beautiful mountains are named for the blue haze that settles in the deep valleys and glazes the peaks, which were heaved up from the sea bed about 25 million years ago.

The mountains are 45km (28 miles) east to west, 19km (12 miles) north to south, and rise precipitously to reach 2,256m (7,402ft) at Blue Mountain Peak. Copious rainfall feeds lush epiphytes and bromeliads. Ferns, palms, bamboo and mahogany cling to the precipitous slopes. Gnarled elfin forest and alpine meadows are found at higher elevations.

The **Blue Mountains and John Crow National Park** (79,126 hectares/195,527 acres) was established to protect what remains of these ancient forests, which still resound with bird calls.

Anyone prepared to negotiate the snaking roads can wind from sea level to mountain peak in less than an hour to enter this realm of clouds and greenery and breathtaking views.

Keep in mind temperature drops significantly with altitude and take a sweater along.

The Cooperage

The name is literal. The place, 3.2km (2 miles) north of Papine, takes its name from the Irish coopers who constructed wooden barrels for the export of rum. The coopers lived up the hill in Irish Town.

Cinchona Botanical Gardens

Cinchona clings spectacularly to a ridge top at over 1,500m (5,000ft) elevation. The magnificent mountaintop views alone make the arduous journey worthwhile.

Cinchona, 4.8km (3 miles) east of Clydesdale, was established in 1868 as a plantation growing Assam tea and cinchona trees, from the bark of which the anti-malaria drug quinine is extracted. But the plantation proved unprofitable and gradually died out. Cinchona was tranformed into an English-style botanical garden.

A wide variety of imported trees and plants that grow here include rhododendrons and azaleas that blaze brightly in spring. Dazzlingly colourful lilies bloom in summer. The Great House at the top of the garden is fronted by well-tended lawns.

You will need a sturdy four-wheel-drive vehicle; the alternative is to hike.

Hollywell Recreational Park

Though it was set up to protect a hauntingly beautiful montane cloud forest, Hollywell, 3.2km (2 miles) north of Newcastle, also functions as a natural bird sanctuary. Bird song fills the mist-shrouded pine forest. Wild strawberries and ferns grow in exuberant abundance amongst the undergrowth. Though Hurricane Ivan demolished many trees (*see p7*), Hollywell has since been extensively replanted.

The sanctuary has many marked trails. One leads to a promontory overlooking the city. There are three rustic cabins for hire and two attractive campsites in the park. Contact the JCDT (Jamaican Conservation and Development Trust) for details.
Tel: (876) 960 2848;
www.greenjamaica.org.jm

Mavis Bank

This small mountain town is built around Jamaica's oldest working coffee factory: the **Mavis Bank Coffee Factory** (JABLUM Jamaica Ltd), owned by Keble Munn, former Minister of Agriculture. The pulpery is supplied by small-scale coffee producers scattered throughout the mountains (*see also p44*).
Factory tours are offered during regular opening hours. To check timings, tel: (876) 977 8005;
www.exportjamaica.org

Newcastle

Newcastle is a Jamaica Defence Force training camp that allows access to tourists. The cantonment clambers up the hillside from 1,000 to 1,400m (3,500–4,500ft) elevation. The parade ground, bisected by the main road, has a cannon, plus the insignia of Jamaica regiments on the wall.
It offers fantastic views down the mountainside to Kingston. With luck, your arrival may coincide with a military parade.

A trail marked 'Woodcutters Gap' leads from the road above the camp through an area of wild ginger lilies, tree ferns and lush forest.
The Blue Mountains rise immediately north of Kingston and extend 40km (25 miles) eastward. The administrative office of the Blue Mountains region, which offers advice on exploring the area, is situated in Hollywell recreational park (see opposite).

Mountains as far as the eye can see: the view from the hill town of Mavis Bank

Hike: Blue Mountains

For the hardy and adventurous nature lover, few experiences in Jamaica can top the hike to Blue Mountain Peak (2,254m/7,395ft). It is moderately strenuous and usually accomplished in the very early morning hours while still dark. The sunrise, the views as the whole of Jamaica appears in the morning light, and the flora and fauna make for a sublime experience.

Allow 7 to 8 hours for the round trip from Whitfield Hall.

Trails from Mavis Bank and Hagley Gap (both reachable by car) lead to Penlyn Castle and thence to Whitfield Hall and Abbey Green, where the Blue Mountain Peak trail starts. It is 1,036m (3,400ft) and 10km (6 miles) from Abbey Green to the summit. Abbey Green can also be reached by jeep via Hagley Gap, the closest village to the peak.

Plan on staying at one of the guesthouses/hostels and setting off for the summit before 4am to avoid the clouds that set in by mid-morning. A guide is recommended.

From Hagley Gap

Follow the dirt road that leads left from the village square towards Penlyn Castle.

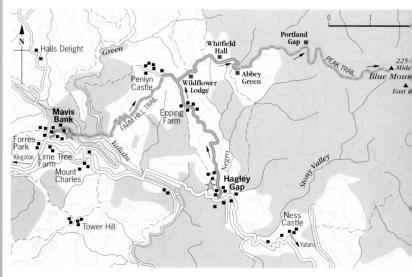

Bearing right, continue past Whitfield Hall to Abbey Green (7km/4 miles).

From Mavis Bank

Follow the steep, narrow footpath to Penlyn Castle (9km/5½ miles). A local can point the way. From there, leave the Post Office (on your right) and follow the road past Wildflower Lodge and Whitfield Hall to Abbey Green (2.5km/1½ miles).

The path to the summit is clearly marked, though lined with thick foliage. It switchbacks steeply through fountain-like glades of bamboo and ferns. Above 1,650m (5,500ft) are stunted, gnarled trees – a rare remnant of cloud forest – festooned with mosses and epiphytes. The only sounds are chirrups and peepings of insects and frogs; the only lights are the phosphorescence of blinkies and peeny wally beetles, and occasional views of Kingston twinkling like a galaxy far below.

Windswept scrub commands the flat-topped summit, where there is a small hut. It will be chilly, with a strong wind.

The sunrise alone is worth the hike. As the sun crests the horizon, ridge after mountain ridge emerges, and on a clear day you should be able to see Cuba to the north.

Do not dally at the top. There is much to admire as you descend: colourful birds and butterflies, dwarf orchids, honeysuckle, rhododendrons, and the pendulous blossoms of 'Jamaican rose' (merianias) that seem to glow from within when struck by sunlight.

Accommodation

There are two attractive places to stay in Mavis Bank which both organise tours and provide guides to the peak:
Forres Park: wooden cabins. Meals available on request.
Tel: (876) 927 8275; www.forrespark.com
Lime Tree Farm: spacious cottages on working coffee farm several kilometres above Mavis Bank with all meals included in the rates.
Tel: (876) 881 8788;
www.limetreefarm.com

Two hostels between Penlyn and Abbey Green provide basic dormitory accommodation and kitchen facilities: **Wildflower Lodge** (*tel: (876) 929 5395*) and **Whitfield Hall** (*tel: (876) 927 0986*).

The Forestry Department maintains a shelter at Portland Gap (3.5km/ 2¼ miles beyond Abbey Green).

When to go

December to April and June to September provide the best hiking weather. However, it can rain on any day of the year and the weather can change hour by hour. May, and late September to October, are the rainiest months.

What to take

It can be cool by day and cold at night, so bring a sweater and/or jacket, plus rain gear. The terrain is rugged and slippery in places; wear sturdy shoes or boots. Take plenty of food, water and a torch.

Drive: Blue Mountains

Off this circle are trails, forest reserves, interesting houses, coffee plantations and gardens. The roads are deeply pot-holed (a Jeep is preferable), but the fabulous views make amends. There are few signposts; check your directions with locals. An early start is essential to avoid the mid-morning clouds that settle over the Blue Mountains. Drive with care; the narrow roads hug the mountains. Use the horn on bends.

Allow 5–6 hours, including stops.

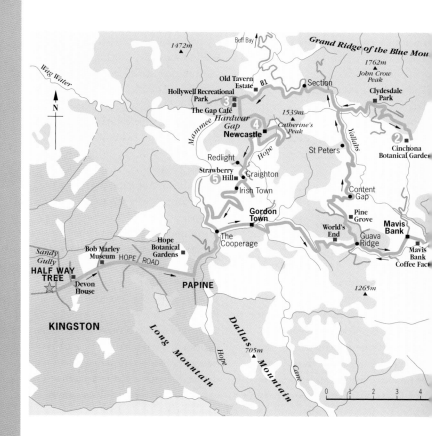

Start at Half Way Tree. Follow Hope Rd past Devon House, the Bob Marley Museum and Hope Botanical Gardens. Keep left at Papine. After about 10km (6 miles), turn right at the The Cooperage, past Gordon Town, World's End and right at Guava Ridge to the Mavis Bank Coffee Factory.

1 Mavis Bank Coffee Factory

This is Jamaica's oldest coffee factory (*see p39*).

Return to Guava Ridge. Turn right at the sign for Pine Grove. Beyond St Peters is a junction for Clydesdale. Turn right; it is a rough drive or a 2-hour hike to Cinchona.

2 Cinchona Botanical Gardens

Founded in 1868 to grow cinchona trees (the bark of this tree produces quinine used to combat malaria), the gardens cling to a mountaintop ridge. Rhododendrons and azaleas are seen at their best in spring, while lilies bloom in abundance in early summer.

Return via Clydesdale to the junction. Turn right for Section, where the road joins the B1. Bear left for Hardwar Gap. After about 5km (3 miles), the entrance to Hollywell National Forest is on your right.

3 Hollywell Recreational Park

Part of the Blue Mountains and John Crow National Park, Hollywell has one of the few remaining montane forests in Jamaica. There are picnic spots and trails. *Tel: (876) 960 2848.*

Banana plantations on the Blue Mountains

Stop for refreshment at the Gap Café (tel: (876) 997 3032; closed Mon), then follow the B1 south to Newcastle.

4 Newcastle

This military camp, established in 1841, nestles idyllically on the mountainside. The parade ground, replete with cannon and regimental insignia, offers a spectacular view over Kingston.

The road drops steeply past Craighton Estate. Below Redlight, follow the sign right up a steep, forbidding road to Strawberry Hill.

5 Strawberry Hill

This restored 17th-century Great House is now a luxurious plantation-style hotel and restaurant where guests can enjoy a splendid 360-degree view.

Tel: (876) 944 8400; www.islandoutpost.com

Continue downhill through Irish Town, named after the Irish coopers who constructed the rum barrels in the 19th century. Turn right at The Cooperage for Kingston.

Blue Mountain coffee

Jamaica's Blue Mountains are a promised land for the coffee tree, which here produces beans of world-famed quality. The angle and aspect of the well-drained slopes, together with the subtle combinations of minerals, sunshine and cool mountain mists, conspire to produce a healthy berry that gives a full-bodied, aromatic coffee with an exceptionally fine, earthy flavour.

Jamaica's coffee comes from the arabica bean, which is far more flavourful than the robusta bean grown in South America. Coffee *cognoscenti* regard Blue Mountain coffee with something akin to adoration – novelist Ian Fleming, who lived part-time in Jamaica, would not let James Bond, his literary hero, drink any other.

Coffee has been grown in the Blue Mountains since 1728, when the Jamaican governor, Sir Nicholas Lawes, imported seedlings from Martinique. Cultivation spread quickly. The boom quickened following the revolution in Haiti in 1790, when many skilled coffee growers fled to Jamaica. By 1840, coffee exports had risen to over 17,000 tonnes a year.

With the final abolition of slavery in 1838, decline set in. By 1951, when a

Emptying the sacks of coffee beans

hurricane sheared most of the plants off the mountains, the industry was almost dead.

In 1973, the Jamaican government established the Coffee Industry Board to stimulate the dying industry. Strict quality controls were enacted, and the government regulated the Blue Mountain coffee name.

Today, about 11,300 hectares (28,000 acres) are devoted to coffee cultivation, but only 9,000 are legally within the bounds of the Blue Mountain parameters: above 610m (2,000ft). The richest, mildest coffee grows near the plant's uppermost

Tasting the final product

the Coffee Industry Board or roasted (often over a smoky wood fire) and vacuum-sealed to retain the fragrance characteristic of Blue Mountain coffee.

Almost the entire crop is exported to Japan, where Blue Mountain coffee is a status symbol and pampered palates are prepared to pay up to £8 a cup (many of the few large plantations that exist are owned by Japanese companies, which invested heavily in the Jamaican coffee industry in the early 1980s).

altitudinal limits, where the bean takes longer to mature. Other coffee beans are known as High Mountain Blend, or Lowland, depending on their origin.

The pulperies (processing plants) are supplied by more than 4,000 small- and medium-sized farms scattered throughout the mountains. In April, with the first rains, small white blossoms burst forth and the air is laced with jasmine-like perfume. By November, the glossy, 2m- (6½ft-) tall bushes are plump with shiny red berries.

The hand-picked berries are trucked or carried by donkey to the pulperies, where they are scrubbed, washed, dried and then sorted according to size and shape before being sold to

Preparing for export

Castleton Botanical Gardens

Follow the twisting A3 north 32km (20 miles) from Kingston to reach this fascinating showcase of 1,000 species of native and exotic plants, high in the mountains. The 6-hectare (15-acre) garden slopes down to the Wag Water River and is well watered by heavy rain.

The gardens were established in 1862 and quickly grew to become the most richly stocked in the Caribbean. Though Hurricane Gilbert battered this lush Eden severely, the huge tree ferns, azaleas, 35 species of palms, and such local plants as strychnos (from which strychnine poison is derived) are worth viewing. The densest exhibits are on the left side of the road.

Open: daily 6am–6pm. Admission free, but guides expect tips.

The amazing Pride of Burma is just one of the blooms at Castleton Botanical Gardens

Port Royal

Relics of Jamaica's most colourful past come alive in Port Royal, the old pirate capital at the tip of the Palisadoes Peninsula, south of Kingston.

The English built a fort here in 1656. Encouraged by the government, buccaneers made the settlement their base for strikes against Spanish ports and ships. Port Royal was soon awash with ale houses and whores – a Babylon of debauchery with the sobriquet 'wickedest city in the world'. It seemed like a divine judgement when, on 7 June 1692, an earthquake and tidal wave toppled two-thirds of it into the harbour.

Though rebuilt and maintained by the British Navy as their West Indian headquarters throughout the 18th century, the town never regained its former stature. Today it is a dilapidated fishing village with a reputation for serving up excellent fried fish. A long-touted restoration has yet to get under way.

Attractions are open daily 9am–5pm. Since the ferry service from Kingston was discontinued in 2004, the only way to reach Port Royal is by car or city bus no 98.

Fort Charles

Most impressive of Port Royal's attractions is this landlocked, red-brick fort that was originally surrounded by water. Many of the 104 cannons that pointed to sea in its heyday can still be seen in their embrasures.

British naval hero Horatio Nelson (1758–1805) served as commander here when only 20 years old. You can tread in his footsteps on the wooden quarterdeck where he walked, warily watching for a French invasion fleet. A plaque tells visitors to 'remember his glory'.

In the centre is a small but charming **Maritime Museum** containing ship models and intriguing nautical paraphernalia. The Grog Shop offers snacks, drinks and souvenirs.
Open: daily 9am–5pm. Admission charge.

Giddy House

On the foreshore in front of the fort is the old Royal Artillery store, up-ended by the earthquake of 1907. It leans at an angle that mildly disorients those stepping inside. Nearby is a huge gun emplacement with a massive cannon lying impotent to the side.

Lime Cay

Some dozen coral cays lie offshore south of Harbour Head spit. Fringed by snow-white sand and shallow turquoise waters, these tiny uninhabited islets are perfect for snorkelling and sunbathing. Lime Cay is popular with Kingstonians who picnic here at weekends. Nude bathing is common. The Morgan's Harbour Hotel offers transportation.

St Peter's Church

This rather drab building, erected in 1725, is intriguing for the stranger-than-fiction tale of Lewis Galdye Esq, whose gravestone you may spy in the church entrance. The aged slab tells how Galdye 'was swallowed up in the Great Earth-quake in the Year 1692 & By the Providence of God was by another Shock thrown into the Sea & Miraculously saved by swimming until a Boat took him up'. Note the silver plate said to have been taken from the sack of Panama City by Henry Morgan.

Port Royal Maritime Museum

48

Walk: Port Royal

This straightforward walk takes in the major historic sites that reflect Port Royal's glory years as the most important city in the Caribbean. You will also get to see something of the local lifestyle that lends Port Royal a funky charm.

Allow 1½ hours.

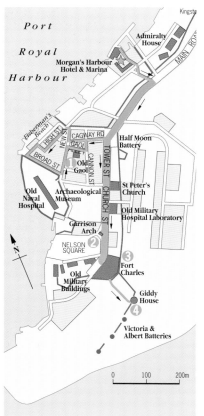

Begin at Morgan's Harbour Hotel and Marina. Exit, turn right and follow the old dockyard wall to Cagway Rd. At the end, cross the public square. Turn left on High St and follow it to Fisherman's Beach, where pirogues and nets festoon the sand. Turn left up Broad St and left to reach Gaol Alley.

1 Old Gaol

The sturdy stone gaol, which predates the 1692 earthquake, has been restored but is closed to the public.
Turn left at the junction of Gaol Alley and Cannon St. Turn right on to Cagway Rd and right on Tower St. Note the parapets on the town wall, and Half Moon Battery on your left. Continue past St Peter's Church and the Garrison Arch to Nelson Sq.

2 Nelson Square

The old parade ground is lined with barrack buildings, many of which still reflect the damage done in 1988 by Hurricane Gilbert.

3 Fort Charles

The solid, well-preserved red-brick fort is replete with cannons. A maritime museum is housed in one of the restored buildings in the fort's courtyard (*see p46*).

Exit the fort at its southwest corner and follow the trail to Giddy House and the Victoria and Albert Batteries.

4 Giddy House

This lopsided building that used to be the Royal Artillery store keeled over during the 1907 earthquake and has stayed that way since – hence its very appropriate name. Behind is a line of gun batteries, with massive cannons still intact (*see p47*).

Return to Morgan's Harbour Hotel and Marina.

Walk: Port Royal

The appropriately named Giddy House

The east

Jamaica's far east should be flush with tourists. It is not, though it was the island's first resort region and has a long history of celebrity patronage. The rich and famous still relax here. Nowadays the Windward Coast's slow pace and easy charm have attracted an eclectic group of mostly European expats who run some of the most charming hotels in Jamaica.

A sense of near-perfect inaccessibility protects this staggeringly beautiful corner from mass tourism. That, and the rains. The area receives three times as much rain as Montego Bay and Ocho Rios (to be fair, it generally falls at night). Hurricane Gilbert swept through it in September 1988,

East Jamaica

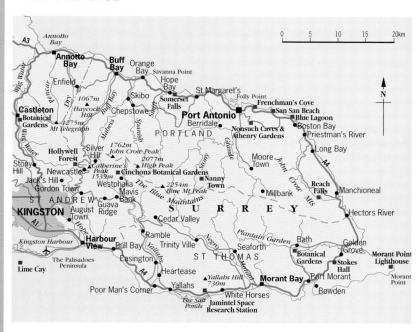

destroying vegetation and roads. The roads were repaired only to be damaged again in 2004 by Hurricane Ivan. Now they are part of an extensive island-wide road-building programme, though for the moment they remain woefully pot-holed. Vegetation damaged in both hurricanes has fared better and is once more gloriously green and tropical. Giant ferns and bamboo brush against your car, and the hills that rise towards the serried John Crow and cloud-covered Blue Mountains are buried under tumbles of plumbagos, morning glory and poinsettias.

No coral reef protects this windward shore. The road rises, dips and curves past wave-chewed rocky headlands. Deep bays beckon surfers – Boston Bay and Long Bay are the finest. Lonely fishing villages are tucked in the coves. The south-facing shores are more sheltered and lined with beautiful, expansive beaches east of Morant.

Diversions are many. In the 1960s rafting the Rio Grande by moonlight was considered the quintessence of romance… until, that is, a formally dressed party tipped unceremoniously over into the water. However, you can still find amusement rafting Jamaica's longest river by day. Reach Falls and Somerset Falls provide refreshing distractions, as do Nonsuch Caves (pretty and generally free of tourist buses). Crystal Springs, a quasi-botanical garden, has several fine specimens. Off the beaten path, Bath, surrounded by fields of sugar cane as green as ripe limes, also has a botanical garden, plus piping-hot mineral springs.

Game fishing is another prime attraction – if the lure strikes, head out into the indigo ocean to hunt a blue marlin in what are the island's finest fishing grounds.

Alternatively, you may wish simply to settle in quaint Port Antonio or one of the nearby private coves and while away your days contemplating the mysterious and welcome lack of tourists in this little-known corner of the island.

Just one of the views from the aptly named Bonnie View Hotel, Port Antonio. Informal and relaxed, the town is less commercialised than the big resort towns on the north coast

Port Antonio

Movie hero Errol Flynn, who settled here when his yacht washed ashore, described Port Antonio as 'more beautiful than any woman I've ever seen'. Latter-day tourists may be surprised at this. A first pass through this sleepy, melancholic backwater can invoke a numb 'we've-made-a-terrible-mistake' expression. Persevere and you will soon understand why Port Antonio, a two-hour drive from Kingston or Ocho Rios, is the favoured holiday destination for tourists with insider knowledge as well as Jamaicans escaping the big resort hustle.

During the late 19th century Port Antonio was a bustling banana port. Around 1890, Captain Lorenzo Dow Baker, founder of the Boston Fruit Company, shipped bananas out and began bringing tourists from cold New York City in. Hotels sprouted and Port Antonio was launched as the first tourist resort in Jamaica. A Who's Who of unwinding internationals adopted the town, such as financier J P Morgan, film star Bette Davis, author Rudyard Kipling and, later, Errol Flynn. The wild parties that Flynn hosted here are no more, but night owls must check out the Roof Club. The cruise ships long

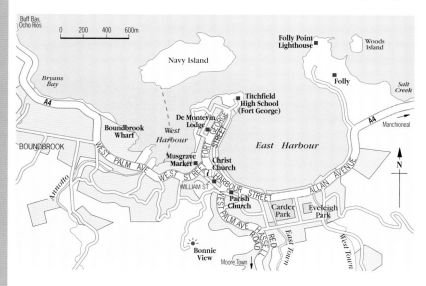

ago decamped to livelier Ocho Rios. And though they still load bananas down at Boundbrook Wharf, that candle, too, barely flickers.

Today, Port Antonio, 108km (67 miles) east of Ocho Rios, is a low-key yet still modern maritime harbour. The genteel lifestyle does linger, though, at sumptuous hotels – most of which are hidden in their own secret coves – where the waiters still call female guests 'm'lady'.

It takes no more than two hours to walk and see Port Antonio. The town nestles between two scenic harbours with garbage-strewn beaches. A good way to get your bearings is from atop the hill south of town.

A walk down the two main streets – Harbour and West streets – will give you a sense of provincial Jamaican life; do call in at Musgrave Market, a great place to buy craft work. Tread carefully or you will disturb the goats that snooze beneath the clock tower in front of the Courthouse.

Before exploring further afield, peek in Christ Church, a prim, red-brick edifice that dominates Port Antonio. Then visit the new marina, with its shops, restaurants, yacht slips and cruise-ship terminal. The town's Victorian-style gingerbread houses are woebegone, the De Montevin Lodge being a noteworthy example.

Port Antonio is a popular film set – it is supposed to have featured in more films than anywhere else in the Caribbean, among them *Lord of the Flies*, *Mighty Quinn*, *Club Paradise* and *Cocktail*.

The town's greatest assets are the tiny, talc-textured beaches east of the town, and the game fish that swim not too far out to sea (the prestigious Port Antonio Blue Marlin Tournament is held each October). Oh, yes, and the lack of tourism is precisely what makes Port Antonio so appealing.

The Jamaica Tourist Board office (tel: (876) 993 3051) is located upstairs at City Centre Shopping Plaza, on Harbour St.

Port Antonio harbour: quiet, now that the film stars have sailed away

Blue Lagoon

The Blue Lagoon is a 55m- (180ft-) deep cup in the coast, actually a limestone sinkhole filled with deep azure waters. The beauty spot, 8km (5 miles) east of Port Antonio, is surrounded by deep-green jungle. It is fed by freshwater springs that seep up into the salt-water lagoon.

The lagoon, locally called 'Blue Hole', is good for swimming and snorkelling. Locals will gleefully tell you, quite incorrectly, that Errol Flynn dived to the bottom.

Yes, the movie *Blue Lagoon* was filmed here. *Club Paradise* was also filmed here. Due to a land dispute, the Waterside Restaurant complex is now closed and there are no changing facilities nor water-sports operators at the site. You can still swim in the lagoon's crystal-clear waters, of course – admission is officially free, though local hustlers may try and charge you.

Bonnie View

Drive up Richmond Hill for this landmark view. The property (unfortunately, rather run-down these days) is perched on a promontory that offers a splendid 360-degree view over the town, coast and Blue Mountains.

Clear blue waters give the Blue Lagoon its name

The 10-hectare (25-acre) grounds are good for horse riding.

Boundbrook Wharf

Boundbrook Wharf, on West Harbour, was once the main deep-water pier of the United Fruit Company, and inspiration for Harry Belafonte's 'Banana Boat Song'.

Today there are no stevedores 'working all night on a drink of rum' or waiting for the tallyman to tally their bananas. But you can still see bananas being loaded on to boats bound for Europe and North America.

Christ Church

This neo-Romanesque, red-brick Anglican church at the east end of Harbour Street was built in 1840. It is impressive within and has a brass lectern donated by the Boston Fruit Company in 1900.
West Palm Ave and Harbour St.

De Montevin Lodge

You do not need to stay at De Montevin Lodge to appreciate its homely beauty. The red-brick, gingerbread-trimmed guesthouse boasts carved hardwood doorways and staircase, impressive coloured tilework, Tiffany lamps, and chintz sofas that will remind you of grandma's old parlour.

The structure was built as a town house by the Hon David Gideon, Custos of Portland Parish at the turn of the 20th century.
Titchfield St.

Fort George

Fort George, on the peninsula which divides East and West Harbour, dates from 1729. In its heyday it was one of the most powerful forts in the Caribbean.

Since 1875 it has been occupied by the Titchfield High School, whose playground was once the military parade ground. The tip of the promontory, behind the school, was the bastion – you can still see embrasures for 22 cannons in its 3m- (10ft-) thick walls. A few of the cannons still remain.

Folly

Follow the headland east of East Harbour and you will reach a pseudo-Grecian estate lying roofless under the sun. The shell is that of a 60-room mansion built in 1905 by an American millionaire, Alfred Mitchell, for his lady love, a Tiffany heiress. Alas, says local legend, he used seawater in the cement, causing the structure to quickly dissolve. Castle and lady both disappeared, leaving only a legendary ruin, appropriately called Folly.

The dour, evocative structure is a favoured setting for music videos and magazine shoots. The Folly Point Lighthouse, built in 1888, can be climbed for fine views of the town and Woods Island, immediately east. When Mitchell stocked it with monkeys, it became known as Monkey Island; however, no monkeys remain. You can swim out or take a boat.

Frenchman's Cove

This cosy little cove, 3km (2 miles) east of town, protects a boutique beach where you may bathe topless. A gin-clear stream winds lazily between the lava-rock headlands and spills on to the beach.

In the 1950s, a millionaire built what was acclaimed as the most expensive hotel in the world atop the cliffs. For a while, Frenchman's Cove was a place where royalty soaked up the sun. The hotel barely functions these days and you may find that you even have the beach to yourself. *Admission charge.*

Port Antonio Marina and Boat Yard

This new marina, pride of Port Antonio and recently named the Errol Flynn Marina to celebrate the town's most famous resident, offers restaurants, a gift shop and Internet access, as well as a 32-slip mega-yacht facility and small cruise-ship terminal (*www.errolflynnmarina.com*).

There are long-standing plans to develop Navy Island, Errol Flynn's old playground, into an up-market hotel resort. You may be able to persuade a local fisherman to take you there.

San San Beach, where the rich play

The enticing golden sands and azure sea of secluded Frenchman's Cove

San San Beach

Eight kilometres (5 miles) east of Port Antonio is the half-moon bay of San San Beach. Talcum-fine sand, and calm aquamarine sea with some of the area's best snorkelling, make San San one of the loveliest beaches in Portland. It's used by the guests of several up-market hotels nearby, though non-guests are also welcome. The stairway to the beach descends through thick, wild greenery. The beach is backed by a golf course (9-hole), hacked from the overgrown valley with machetes.

Offshore is Pellew Island, which a wealthy socialite – Baron Heinrich Thyssen – gave as a honeymoon gift to his wife.

Open: daily 9am–5pm. Admission charge.

ERROL FLYNN

In 1947, film hero Errol Flynn washed up in Jamaica when his yacht *Zacca* was blown ashore by a storm. Quite taken with the place – 'When God created Eden, this is what he was aiming at,' he wrote – Flynn bought Navy Island, as well as the Titchfield Hotel, a watering hole for the likes of Rudyard Kipling, and even a cattle ranch on Priestman's River.

Flynn swashbuckled his way around Jamaica in typical Hollywood fashion. He organised raft races on the Rio Grande and threw wild parties that are the stuff of local legend. His beguiling ways attracted other Hollywood stars. This select bunch put Port Antonio and Jamaica on the map.

In a way, Flynn never left. It is easy to imagine the sun-bronzed screen idol strolling along the beach, hair tousled by the wind and trousers rolled up, on his way for a drink.

Annotto Bay

Sleepy, ramshackle Annotto Bay straggles along the coast, midway between Ocho Rios and Port Antonio, at the junction of the road across the Blue Mountains to Kingston. An old train station, now disused, once bustled during the banana boom when Annotto handled the produce from 48 estates.

Take time to peek inside the slightly baroque-style Baptist Church, near the market square. The yellow-and-red brick structure, built in 1894 according to a plaque, has intriguing decorative plaster motifs.

The town is named after an orange dye made from the seeds of the *bixa orellana*, or anatta tree, used by Arawak Indians for body paints.

Nonsuch Caves and Athenry Gardens

Well-lit concrete pathways lead through nine chambers formed long before Jamaica rose above the sea – fish and other sea creatures swam through the dark depths, as evidenced by the fossils found there.

Bats hang from the lofty ceiling in the Cathedral or Bat Romance Room, which accurately portrays what goes on. Your guide will conjure up imaginative forms from the coral formations: a bishop, a man in robes upon a camel, even a naked woman emerging from a shell. Emerge from the darkness of the caves to explore Athenry Gardens.

Sci-fi-size heliconia, poinciana and bird of paradise blossom madly in these neatly tended gardens on a 75ha

The Cathedral, one of the Nonsuch Caves discovered in 1955

(185-acre) coconut plantation high in the hills overlooking Port Antonio. The cafeteria offers refreshing beer and soft drinks; its pavilion provides intoxicating views.

Nonsuch, 6.5km (4 miles) south of Port Antonio. Tel: (876) 779 7144. Open on cruise-ship days 9am–5pm. Admission charge.

Bath

During Victorian days, Bath was the most fashionable resort in Jamaica. Today it is worth a visit for two singular attractions that remain unchanged. Then, as now, it was surrounded by lush sugar-cane fields and, to the north, the soaring peaks of the Blue Mountains, from the base of which burble steaming hot springs.

The springs were discovered in 1699 when a slave who had been wounded in seeking his freedom was healed after bathing in the pools. The government appointed the directors of the Bath of St Thomas the Apostle to oversee the administration of the baths. Accommodation was built in 1747 and 30 slaves were purchased to maintain the road.

Bath Botanical Gardens

The arboretum and garden, next to Bath's venerable white-stone church, were the island's first. Planted in 1779, the gardens have since shrunk in size, though they remain of great charm. Many of Jamaica's imported plants first took root here, including bougainvillaea, cinnamon, jacaranda, and the breadfruit brought from the South Seas by Captain William Bligh. *76km (47 miles) east of Kingston.*

Bath Fountain Hotel

This colonial-style hotel (*tel: (876) 703 4345*), 3km (2 miles) north of town, still has natural hot-spring baths open to the casual visitor, as well as accommodation and a restaurant. A 20-minute soak will supposedly cure all your ills.

Alternatively, a rough path rises along the embankment opposite the hotel that leads to the undeveloped and 'public' hot springs. Accept a guide, who will lead you along the muddy way, past local inhabitants – and heady whiffs of *ganja* – to a stream in a valley. The hot water that emerges from a pipe in the side of the hill allegedly offers the same curative properties as that which flows to the hotel. The guide will offer massages and alternative therapies and, whether accepted or not, will await his tip.

Boston Bay

Your first, idyllic, impression of Boston Bay, 15km (9 miles) east of Port Antonio, is of a wide crescent of white sand enclosed in a pleasing cove. When calm, the water is like a turquoise jewel; when the sea is up, massive waves crash ashore, drawing surfers. There are plenty of water sports to choose from.

This is where Jamaica's commercial 'jerk' legend began. The well-maintained public beach is rimmed by stalls where chicken, lobster and wild boar sizzle in pepper-sauce marinade. Jerk was created by the Maroons who hunted boar in the mountains around. Wild boar are still hunted and on any day you can smell the meat being slow cooked over pimento wood. You can buy some along with puddles of spicy sauce and piles of fried 'festival' dumplings.

The Bath Fountain Hotel where you can soak your ailments away – allegedly

Long Bay

Jamaica's dramatic coastal scenery reaches its zenith at Long Bay, where strong winds forcefully push waves ashore on to two wide, scimitar-shaped beaches backed by palms. It is unfortunate that the deep turquoise waters are marred by an unpredictable undertow. Colourful fishing pirogues draped with nets are drawn up on the beach – perfect roosts for pelicans.

The bay has been adopted by foreigners who lead a laid-back, counter-culture type of life and rent rooms to visitors.

Manchioneal

Manchioneal is a sleepy fishing village, an away-from-it-all place of peace and quiet set in a deep, scalloped bay with calm turquoise waters and a narrow

Cricket is the Jamaican passion: seen here in a rustic setting at Moore Town

beach. Fishing pirogues add a dash of colour. The hamlet is named after the poisonous seaside plant that used to grow here. This is a great place to sample freshly caught fried fish and delicious conch soup.

Moore Town

Lonesome Moore Town is capital of the Windward Maroons (*see p79*). The small village is scattered along the course of a stream 16km (10 miles) south of Port Antonio via a steep, winding dirt road. En route, you may see Maroon descendants carrying bananas in traditional head slings.

The Maroons harassed the British army and plantocracy from their redoubts in the John Crow Mountains for almost a century. In 1734, the British finally flushed the Maroons from their mountain fortress at Nanny Town, and five years later signed a peace treaty which established Moore Town as the Maroons' capital.

Moore Town and its environs are a semi-autonomous political unit (note the Jamaican and Maroon flags that fly together). A Maroon 'Colonel' presides over a committee of 24 elected council members. Village meetings take place on the common or recreation ground, known as *Osofu* (meeting place).

If you're visiting, it's Maroon protocol to 'check in' with the current Colonel – ask in the village for his whereabouts. He will also be able to find decent local guides, should you want to explore further afield.

Bump Grave

The simple stone monument opposite
the school is Bump Grave, where,
according to legend, the remains of
Maroon leader Nanny are buried.
Nanny was imbued with supernatural
powers. It was recorded that she
'received the bullets of the enemy that
were aimed at her, and returned them
with fatal effect, in a manner of which
decency forbids a nearer description'.
The government declared her a
national heroine in 1975 and erected
the memorial.

The church at Moore Town

Morant Bay

Follow the coast road east from Port
Antonio and you will eventually reach
the town of Morant Bay, on the
southeast coast. In the town square is a
statue of Paul Bogle, a Jamaican
preacher hanged by the British in the
aftermath of the 1865 Morant Bay
rebellion. The statue is the work
of the Honourable Edna Manley,
wife and mother of former Jamaican
prime ministers.

Bogle had led a protest march during
a period of unemployment and poverty
when tensions ran high. The authorities
fired into the crowd, inciting a riot in
which 28 people were killed and the
courthouse burned down. Martial law
was declared, thousands of men and
women were flogged, and 430 were
executed in reprisal for the rioting.
A Royal Commission found that the
punishment was 'positively barbarous'.
The British parliament reacted by

dissolving the Jamaican House of
Assembly, and Jamaica was named a
Crown Colony.

Morant Bay Fort, behind the rebuilt
courthouse, dates from 1773. It still has
cannons and a park containing the
graves of 78 of the victims executed in
1865. The town's red-brick Anglican
Christ Church dates from 1881.

Morant Point Lighthouse

A red-and-white-hooped lighthouse
marks Morant Point, below Holland
Bay, Jamaica's easternmost headland.

The cast-iron edifice, built in 1841,
is reached from the tumbledown village
of Golden Grove along muddy tracks
that meander through the canefields
of the Tropicana Sugar Estates. Hire
a guide!

The lighthouse keeper shows the
way 30m (100ft) to the top. It is
windy up here, but the impressive
view and the silence make for a
profound experience.

Reach Falls

At Manchioneal, a paved road (a great relief after the pitted main highway) leads inland and climbs through the foothills of the John Crow Mountains to secluded Reach Falls. Following a land dispute, the falls are currently officially closed and there are no facilities available to the public. Even the Rastas who sold tams, necklaces and carved calabash gourds have gone. However, there are always local guides hanging round the entrance who will take you in the 'back way' for a small charge.

A path leads downhill past a mossy cliff face to the tumbling river. The falls cascade high-spiritedly from one jade-coloured pool to another. You may plunge into the effervescent waters, but note the sign that warns: 'Beware of deep pools and strong currents'. A half-mile hike upriver leads to a whirlpool inside Mandingo Cave.

Rio Grande

The island's largest river is also its oldest tourist attraction. Local farmers once floated bananas downstream to St Margaret's Bay, 7km (4 miles) west of Port Antonio. When film hero Errol Flynn arrived (*see p57*), he organised raft races and took his friends rafting – it is said that he used to make the trip twice a day, but never with the same lady!

The ride from Berridale to the river mouth, navigating shoals and steep-sided gorges, is still a favourite with tourists. The journey takes about three hours. En route, you will glide past rustic villages and some of the loveliest scenery in Jamaica. Riverside vendors, even musicians, serve the river traffic. It is very romantic, especially on full-moon nights.

Trips end at Rafter's Rest, St Margaret's Bay. Rio Grande Attractions Ltd, PO Box 128, Port Antonio. Tel: (876) 993 2778.

Somerset Falls

This pleasing picnic and hiking spot, 2km (1¼ mile) east of Hope Bay, is set in a cool, shady canopy where the Daniels River cascades through lush

The beautiful Reach Falls

A farmer stands in front of the ruins of 17th-century Stokes Hall

forest. A raftsman will pole you to the base of the falls, where you may plunge Tarzan-like from a high rock. All around, ginger lilies, heliconia and wild bananas grow in profusion.

There are toilets and a small jerk restaurant. An adjacent fish farm, fed by water from the falls, raises silver perch. *Open: daily 9am–5pm. Admission charge.*

Stokes Hall

Three kilometres (2 miles) south of Golden Grove you will see Stokes Hall to the east, sitting atop a hill. The overgrown remains are those of a fortified Great House dating back to the 17th century and built by one of the three sons of Governor of Jamaica Luke Stokes, who died of swamp fever in 1660.

Yallahs

Cattle wander through the streets of ramshackle Yallahs. The village, 32km (20 miles) east of Kingston, sits amid arid scrubland and is in itself of no particular interest.

The wide and usually dry Yallahs River, west of town, washes great swathes of boulders and pebbles over the road during flash floods.

Kach Mansong memorial

On the hillside 10km (6 miles) west of Yallahs is a roadside marker placed by the Jamaican National Heritage Trust in honour of Kach Mansong, or 'Three-finger Jack'.

The tablet tells us that in these hills, between 1780 and 1781, 'he fought, often single-handedly, a war of terror against the English soldiers and planters who held the slave territory. Strong, brave, skilled with machete and musket, his bold exploits were equalled only by his chivalry.' He was ambushed and killed in 1781.

Salt ponds

On the eastern outskirts of Yallahs you will pass by two huge, shallow lakes of soupy water separated from the sea by a narrow spit. These briny ponds teem with brine shrimp and micro-organisms that attract wading birds. They are occasionally used to extract salt and in the 18th century produced 10,000 bushels (364kl) of salt annually.

The ponds often flare bright red. Though legend claims it is the blood of slaves murdered here, it is actually caused by bacteria that bloom during a drought, emitting a powerful stench.

Walk: Port Antonio

A run-down banana port of tropical languor, Port Antonio nonetheless offers a handful of intriguing attractions and two particularly appealing vistas best enjoyed on a walking tour.

Allow 1½ hours, or 2½ hours including Bonnie View.

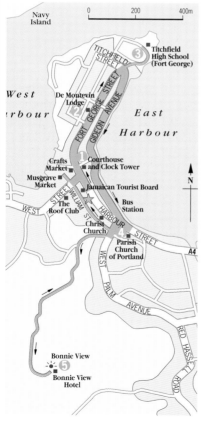

Start at the Jamaica Tourist Board upstairs at City Plaza on Harbour St. You can park across the road in front of the courthouse.

1 Courthouse and clock tower

This handsome red-brick Georgian building is adorned with a cupola and iron verandas. It dominates the main square of the town, which also features a clock tower.

Cross Harbour St at the square's southeast corner and enter the lively Musgrave Market for a quick browse. Return to the square and turn left on Fort George St. Then walk uphill 135m (150yds).

2 De Montevin Lodge

This venerable hotel, former home of an English sea captain, still has mahogany furniture, gingerbread highlights and a quirky charm (tel: (876) 993 2604).

Continue along Fort George St to the end of the peninsula. En route you will pass several quaint houses, some decorated with gingerbread fretwork relics of the town's heyday.

3 Titchfield School (Fort George)

It is difficult to tell where Titchfield School ends and Fort George begins. Parts of the fortifications still stand (the main school building was the old barracks), and there are still several cannons.

Turn right from Fort George St and follow Gideon Ave back into town. The view across the bay towards the Blue Mountains begs a camera. Follow the waterfront to the Jamaica Arcade craft market, on the right. After a brief stop, continue to Harbour St. Turn right. Turn left on to West Palm Ave.

4 Parish Church of Portland

The red-brick Anglican church was built in neo-Romanesque style and completed in 1840.

Continue along West Palm Ave to the five-way junction (note the pretty green-and-ochre wooden building on the left). Turn right on to William St and walk to West St. Turn right and return to the main square.

Alternatively, if hale and hearty, follow the sign for Bonnie View at the five-way junction. The road switchbacks steeply for 0.8km (¹/₂ mile) to the Bonnie View Hotel.

5 Bonnie View Hotel

As the name suggests, the grounds of this hotel have one of the best coastal views in Jamaica (*tel: (876) 993 9970*).

A view of Monkey Island off Port Antonio

Drive: Port Antonio

This off-the-beaten-track drive reveals the 'other side of Jamaica', whose Manchioneal District has been designated by the UN as one of the world's pristine wilderness areas. The road squiggles along a mountain-framed coastline hammered by waves, past sandy coves and through riotous rainforest that hides jewel-like waterfalls. Tourist facilities are meagre.

Allow 8 hours, including stops.

Leave Port Antonio on the A4 heading east. After about 8km (5 miles), San San Beach and Blue Lagoon will be seen on the left.

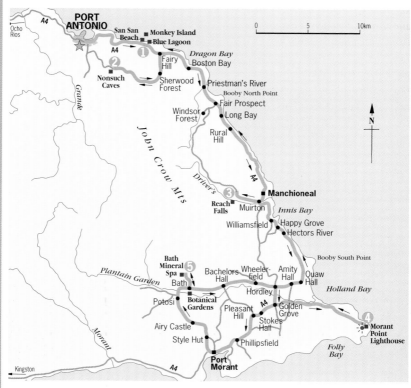

1 San San Beach and Blue Lagoon

A supremely pretty beach backed by several luxurious villas. Good snorkelling on the reef. Pellew Island beckons offshore. Immediately east is Blue Lagoon, a 55m- (180ft-) deep seawater lagoon of deepest azure fed by springs said to have rejuvenating powers on the libido.

0.8km (½ mile) east, turn right at Fairy Hill for Nonsuch Caves.

2 Nonsuch Caves

Nine deep limestone chambers are adorned with stalactites, stalagmites and fossilised sponges. The caves are lit, and traversed by concrete walkways. Bats flit overhead.

Return to Fairy Hill and continuing east you pass a series of beautiful bays. Boston Bay is supposedly where jerk pork was invented. On the left are the Errol Flynn Estates, still run by his widow Patrice Wymore. The John Crow Mountains loom to the right. 0.8km (½ mile) beyond Manchioneal, turn right for Reach Falls.

3 Reach Falls

The crystal waters of the Driver's River cascade over escarpments. The Falls are officially closed but a dip in the cool waters is still possible (*see p62*).

Return to the A4. Continue south past Hectors River, where the road cuts inland through the Tropicana Sugar Estates. Turn left at the crossroads at Hordley. Two kilometres (1 mile) further is Golden Grove. Gluttons for bad roads might turn left at the petrol station after hiring a

The Morant Point Lighthouse

guide to escort them through the canefields to Morant Point Lighthouse.

4 Morant Point Lighthouse

This lonesome, 30m- (100ft-) tall, cast-iron lighthouse – a National Historic Landmark – was fashioned in London in 1841. The keeper will guide you to the top for fabulous views across the plains to the Blue Mountains (*see p38*).

Return to Golden Grove. Turn left for Port Morant. From here, a road to the right winds uphill to Bath. Turn left opposite the Botanical Gardens and follow the winding road for 2.5km (1½ miles).

5 Bath Mineral Spa

This is a popular spa resort, offering private mineral baths that promise a cure for many ills (*tel: (876) 703 4405*). Take a stroll around the botanical gardens nearby.

Continue east 10km (6 miles) to Hordley along a badly potholed road, before you return to Port Antonio.

The north coast

Jamaica's lush north coast is a fusion of green hills and sculptured sand crescents – an idyllic setting for two of the island's prime tourist resorts, Ocho Rios and Runaway Bay. Many of Jamaica's premier sightseeing attractions and natural wonders are concentrated along the north coast between Falmouth and Port Maria.

Further east, the magnificent seascapes build toward a crescendo. The sea, the colour of melted peridot, opens up fully. The craggy coastline is washed by spuming breakers, while the hills that rise towards the Blue Mountains are buried under tumbles of bright-purple plumbagos and flaming heliconias.

The north coast centres on Ocho Rios, long one of the island's most popular holiday spots. Ochi, as Jamaicans call it, spells beaches, water sports, good dining and entertainment, as well as glorious waterfalls and botanical gardens.

The shoreline is lined with cascades such as Dunn's River Falls, an indelible image of Jamaica that is guaranteed to elicit *ooohs* and *aaahs*. When you tire of the beach, you can drive through the lushly majestic Fern Gully, admire orchids and native flowers in botanical gardens, or take an open-air jitney (minibus) or even a horse ride through working plantations.

In its heyday, the north coast was a centre of sugar production. Brimmer

Hall and Prospect Plantation are popular excursion stops that still buzz with activity. Other historic properties, such as Greenwood, near Falmouth, and the site of Sevilla Nueva, near St Ann's, have been restored as museums. One, Good Hope, has been given a new lease of life as a fine hotel in the country.

North-coast Jamaica

The region offers many superlative drives. The road inland from Falmouth to Good Hope, for example, leads to the edge of Cockpit Country – a beautiful and virtually inaccessible jungle-clad region of towering conical hillocks and deep depressions. Following the road south from Runaway Bay brings you to reggae star Bob Marley's mausoleum in Nine Mile, his birthplace in the hills.

East of Ocho Rios the forests thicken. Just down the coast at Oracabessa, novelist Ian Fleming dreamed up James Bond at Goldeneye, now a luxury hotel (and his adventure scenes from *Dr No* were shot hereabouts). Signs point the way to Firefly, dramatist Noël Coward's holiday retreat atop a high promontory above Port Maria. Coward asked to be buried here; you can visit, and understand why.

Runaway and Discovery Bays, long-known for their excellent beaches and scuba diving, are home to several huge new all-inclusive hotels with every visitor need catered for. Sleepy Falmouth, which once buzzed with commerce, still retains some of Jamaica's best-preserved historical gems… and a unique natural curiosity – a phosphorescent lagoon!

The active will find much to enjoy. Chukka Cove offers scenic horse-riding trails, as well as 'soft adventure' tours. There are championship golf courses, and water sports aplenty. You can raft the Martha Brae River. The north coast also boasts some of the best diving and snorkelling in Jamaica; scuba divers can even search for the remains of two worm-ridden ships that Columbus is thought to have scuttled at Sevilla Nueva.

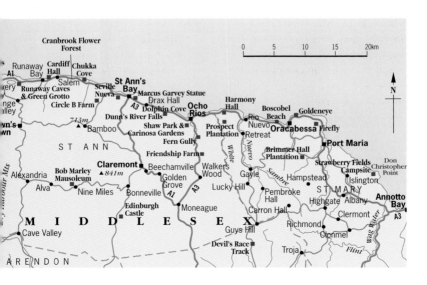

Ocho Rios

Ocho Rios, 108km (67 miles) east of Montego Bay, anchors Jamaica's north coast. It is a 1½-hour drive from Mo'Bay, and a similar jaunt from Kingston over the central mountains. The rambling resort and lively harbour town lies at the foot of an escarpment and enjoys a serene mountain backdrop.

The town wraps around Ocho Rios Bay, which is rimmed by broad beaches. Its position is important – Ochi is a crossroads village where the coast road intersects the road to Moneague and Kingston. Its name, too, is a crossroads – of English and Spanish. Ocho Rios is not Spanish for 'eight rivers', as its name suggests. Rather, it is a corruption of the Spanish word *chorreras* – the waterfalls. In 1657, a Spanish expeditionary force clashed with the English at a site they called Las Chorreras (assumed to be Dunn's River Falls). By 1800, records show the settlement here was officially known as Chorreras; and by 1841 as Ocho Rios.

In the 19th century, Ocho Rios was a centre for pimento production and export. Later years saw decline until assuaged by the arrival of cruise ships and the handful of luxury hotels that came up in the 1960s.

Across the bay is an irrepressibly ugly dock (a now virtually abandoned bauxite-loading facility) where the cruise ships put passengers ashore. Dozens call every month. Then

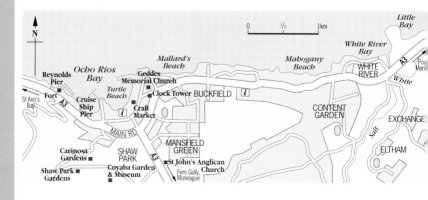

seagoing sightseers storm ashore and overload the restaurants and tourist attractions. Cruise ships tend not to call at weekends. Check the schedule with the town's Tourist Information Office (*tel: (876) 974 7705*).

Ocho Rios is small enough to stroll through in one or two hours, with time added for browsing the native craft stalls. Take a deep breath – the town is unkempt, traffic jams are frequent, hustlers line the pavements, hotels shoulder right up to the in-town beaches, and only occasional hints of sand can be gained as you stroll. In 1996, the City Fathers initiated a clean-up campaign.

There is not too much to see in Ochi, which has little charm and contains only one historic site: the diminutive fort, built in 1777 to defend the town against seafaring invaders. Turtle and Mallard's Beaches more than compensate with their shimmering white sands. The town is, however, heaven for shoppers. Dockside Island Village, with its shops and Reggae Explosion Museum, is excellent for purchases, while nearby Taj Mahal specialises in duty-free goods. Roadsides are lined with craft stalls and rows of duty-free shops sell everything from Swiss watches to *risqué* swimwear. The town also offers a good choice of nightlife for the party crowd (more sedate bars proffer piano, Caribbean theme shows and even karaoke). The choice among restaurants is good – everything from pizza to jerk pork.

Ochi also boasts a widely varied style of hotels, including self-catering villas in the hills above the town, and a selection of de luxe, all-inclusive resorts that are worlds unto themselves. Perched atop their own secluded bays are some of the finest traditional resort hotels in the whole of the Caribbean.

Ocho Rios is a good base for excursions further afield – particularly to Dunn's River Falls, which no one should miss.

For information and maps contact: TPDCO (Tourism Product Development Company) in Ocean Village Plaza, Ocho Rios (*tel: (876) 974 7705*).

High-rises for the many who visit Ocho Rios

Coyaba Gardens and Museum

Coyaba is the Taino name for paradise. Strolling through these tropical gardens bursting with native flora, you may well think you have arrived! You are never far from the mellifluous sound of waterfalls, and fish-filled ponds provide added amusement.

The Spanish-style museum provides an insight into Jamaica's cross-cultural influences and displays the history of Jamaica from Taino days to post-emancipation. An art gallery displays the works of Jamaica's best creative talent. There is a craft shop and a bar serving home-made ginger beer.

Adjacent to Shaw Park Gardens, off the A3. Tel: (876) 974 6235 or 974 4568. Open: daily 8am–5pm. Admission charge.

Dolphin Cove

One of Jamaica's most popular attractions, Dolphin Cove offers visitors the chance to touch and swim with bottlenose dolphins. It's a highly organised operation – it needs to be! There's always a queue for the dolphin experience. While you wait your turn, you can sunbathe on a pretty little beach or refuel at the restaurant and bar. The site also has a small 'Jungle Trail' through the woods, with parrots, snakes and monkeys, and a sea enclosure with stingrays. Booking – at least a fortnight in advance – is essential.

Tel: (876) 974 5335; www.dolphincovejamaica.com. Open: daily 8.30am–5.30pm. Admission charge.

Shaw Park Gardens – a natural haven

Dunn's River Falls

Ocho Rios's most enticing attraction cascades over slippery wedding-cake tiers of limestone to the beach. Joining the daisy chain of tourists who link arms for the 180m (600ft) climb to the top is a must. It is not for the feeble, but is well worth the effort.

Hire one of the sure-footed guides. Rubber-soled wading shoes can also be rented. Remember to take your bathing costume! The roadside ticket booth is at beach level.

The falls are considered the 'Niagara of the Caribbean' – a gross exaggeration, but nonetheless they are exhilarating fun and splendidly photogenic.

Atop the falls, woodcarving souvenir shops display some of the island's best examples of craftsmanship.

On the A3, 3km (2 miles) west of town. Tel: (876) 974 2857. Open: daily 8.30am–5pm; www.dunnsriverja.com. Admission charge.

Island Village and Reggae Explosion

A picturesque development, flanking the Cruise Terminal and catering for disembarking passengers, the complex comprises shops, restaurants, a small beach and a cyber-café. Also within the grounds is Reggae Explosion, an interactive museum celebrating the best of the country's national music. *Tel: (876) 974 8353; www.islandvillageja.com*

Fern Gully

No visit to Ochi is complete without a drive through this sun-dappled nave, located a couple of kilometres south of town. The spectacular 5km (3-mile) journey leads uphill through a world of tropical ferns.

The road follows a dry riverbed that was planted with over 550 native varieties of ferns in the late 19th century. The lush ferns are threatened by noxious traffic fumes that are trapped beneath a canopy of 10m (30ft) tall fern trees.

Fern Gully is now a protected preserve. You may photograph – but no touching, please!

Ocho Rios Fort

The pocket-sized battery with four cannons *in situ* sits next to the disused bauxite-loading terminal west of the town. The fort (built in 1777) did brief duty as a slaughterhouse before being restored in the 1970s by Reynolds Jamaica Mines Ltd.

Shaw Park Gardens

It is a toss-up which is of greater appeal – the superb views over Ocho Rios, or the botanical gardens brimming with exotic and native trees and shrubs. The trills and squawks of birds resound pleasingly. The 10-hectare (25-acre) attraction swathes the high ground south of town, and was originally an attraction of the old Shaw Park Hotel, long since gone.

Off the A3, opposite the Public Library, 2km (1 mile) uphill. Tel: (876) 974 2723; www.shawparkgardens.com. Open: daily 8am–5pm. Admission charge.

Woodcarvings for sale in a shop at Dunn's River Falls

Ocho Rios

Drive: Ocho Rios

There is history and scenic beauty around every bend on this drive combining coast and interior mountains. Inland, the scenery opens up fully into sublime tableaux that will have you begging for more. The route is well paved yet little travelled.

Allow 4–5 hours, including stops.

Leave Ocho Rios westward on the A3, passing the remains of Ocho Rios fort on the right. After about 5km (3 miles), turn left at Dunn's River Falls.

1 Dunn's River Falls

Dunn's River tumbles 180m (600ft) to the beach. Climb it with a guide or admire the view from a walkway (*see*

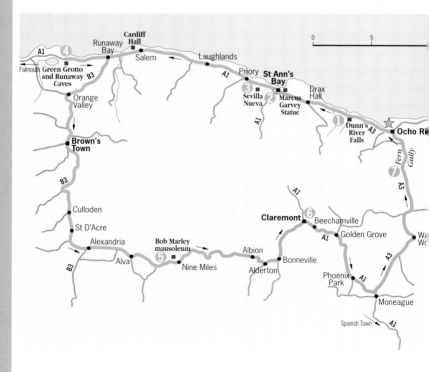

also p72). Continue west along the A3 about 6.5km (4 miles) to St Ann's Bay. Leave the bypass and turn left into town, and left again for the parish library.

2 St Ann's Bay

Marcus Garvey, the father of black nationalism, was born in St Ann's in 1887. A commemorative statue to the national hero stands outside the parish library.

The A3 becomes the A1 west of St Ann's. Follow it for 2km (1 mile) to Seville Great House and Heritage Park.

3 Seville Great House and Heritage Park

Sevilla Nueva was the first Spanish settlement in the New World. Remnants of the fortifications and other structures still stand between the highway and the sea. Across the road is the Sevilla Estate and, on the ridge above, Seville Great House, built in 1745. The site also has Arawak Indian remains (*see also p89*).

Continue west. Runaway Caves are on the left, 3km (2 miles) beyond Runaway Bay.

4 Green Grotto and Runaway Caves

Beautiful stalagmites and stalactites highlight these underground caverns. A guide may coax musical notes from the formations as you enjoy a boat ride through the Green Grotto (*see also p82*).

Return to Runaway Bay. Turn right. The climbing road offers views back over the

coast. After 6.5km (4 miles), turn left at Orange Valley. Continue to Brown's Town and Alexandria. Turn left at the police station. Follow the signs for the Bob Marley Mausoleum.

5 Bob Marley mausoleum, Nine Mile

Reggae superstar Bob Marley lies buried at Nine Mile, the humble village where he was born in 1945. Hustlers are heavy-handed, but a guided tour of Marley's childhood home and mausoleum is interesting.

Continue eastwards through a dramatic landscape of precipitous, jungle-clad hillocks and gorges, then bucolic countryside reminiscent of the Yorkshire Dales. Keep left at Y-junctions at Alderton and Bonneville. Continue to Claremont.

6 Claremont

A somnolent crossroads town whose Wild West-style houses have wooden front pavements. A beautiful old clock tower sits in the centre of town.

Turn right at the clock tower on to the A1. Moneague is 10km (6 miles) away. Turn left here on to the A3. After 14.5km (9 miles), descend through Fern Gully.

7 Fern Gully

A serpentine road descends through this steep-sided gorge lined by lush ferns. Sunlight filters through the canopy, creating a kind of subaqueous light. Craft stalls line the road.

Flags flutter at the entrance to reggae legend Bob Marley's mausoleum at Zion

Bob Marley mausoleum, Nine Mile

A revered site for Rastafarians and reggae fans, the resting place of reggae superstar Bob Marley is fittingly located at his birthplace, Nine Mile, 24km (15 miles) south of Runaway Bay. He died of brain cancer on 11 May 1981.

Zion, the hilltop site of the mausoleum, is where Marley lived as a child. Its preferential position commands dramatic views over the hillocky, forest-clad mountains. The small hut, originally of wood, was rebuilt in stone when the musician was laid to rest. On its walls are the words 'I Bob love jah one love.' Behind the hut is Marley's 'inspiration stone' where he sat and made music and occasionally slept (as recorded in his song 'Rock was my Pillow').

The mausoleum – a tall, oblong block of white Italian marble – is housed in a tiny church of Ethiopian design, surrounded by avocado and mango trees supposedly planted by the young Marley (the family moved to Kingston when he was 13 years old). The rising sun shines on the mausoleum through a stained-glass Star of David window. The interior is decorated with Marley paraphernalia: photos, paintings, 'Ban the Bomb' and 'One Love' stickers, and the like. A tattered black leather book contains thousands of signatures of those in the funeral procession, which reportedly stretched for 80km (50 miles). As you turn the pages, the tears may well!

Artistic hands have graced everything – hut, mausoleum, 'inspiration stone' – in Rasta colours: yellow for sunshine, green for nature's lushness, red for blood. Marley sang of the oneness of mankind, epitomised by his words 'one blood, one love', stressing that the sameness of human blood speaks of the equality of all races regardless of skin colour.

As soon as you arrive, you will be set upon by prospective guides and hustlers, but persevere. A gift shop is full of Marley paraphernalia. A 'jump-up' with live bands is hosted each year on 6 February – Marley's birthday. *Tel: (876) 843 0498; www.ninemile.com; www.bobmarley.com. Open: daily. Admission charge.*

Brimmer Hall

This venerable wooden Great House, near Bailey's Vale, south of Port Maria, is the centrepiece of Brimmer Hall Plantation. The 280-hectare (700-acre) farm gathers bananas, coconuts, sugar cane, citrus and pimento from the lush earth.

A one-hour guided tour by tractor-powered, canopied jitney teaches all about plantation life (intriguing esoterica include how many uses there are for coconuts, and how banana-tree stems are turned into ladies' stockings).

The white-walled house, built about 1817, has an impressive interior. Inside is as cool as a well. Dark hardwoods abound, along with Chinese inlaid hardwood tables, oriental rugs and even an original suit of armour.

You may relax by the swimming pool, where you can sample tropical drinks, curried goat, ackee, salt fish and other local treats. There is also a gift shop. *Brimmer Hall, Port Maria, 6.5km (4 miles) southwest of Port Maria. Tel: (876) 994 2309. Tours: 11am, 1.30pm & 3.30pm. Admission charge.*

The Bob Marley mausoleum

Cockpit Country

Cockpit Country, a virtually townless territory, spreads through southern Trelawny Parish, south of Falmouth. It is an extraordinarily wild and stirringly beautiful region of looming hummocks and flat-bottomed depressions.

Cockpit Country is a classic case of karst topography – where a limestone plateau is dissolved to form deep sinkholes, the 'cockpits' that give the region its name – covering some 1,300sq km (500sq miles) encircled by mountains. The region is riddled with caves that lie dangerously hidden beneath the undulating carpet of thick vegetation.

During colonial days, Maroons – runaway slaves – found refuge here and fought the British to a standstill. Today, the Cockpits are ringed by remote hamlets with peculiar names.

The forbidding region is the least explored in the country. No roads pierce beyond its fringe, though a few make penetrating stabs. Determined hikers can access the region with guides from its main centre, Albert Town to the east. Be warned; the going is extremely rough.

Windsor Caves

On the northern edge of the Cockpit, about 1km ($^2/_3$ mile) south from Windsor Great House, is Windsor Caves. The inconspicuous opening gives no appreciable hint of the grandeur of the chambers within.

The limestone caves are full of stalagmites, stalactites and flowing formations folded like stiff silken drapery. The passageways meander for 3km (2 miles). 'Rooms' range from cavernous to a tight fit. You grope your way forward with a guide who uses the light from a bamboo torch. Cavers can follow a stream that is the source of the Martha Brae.

Take a deep breath before entering – the bat manure gives off quite a stench! The caves are reputedly owned by Lady Rothschild (of the banking family), an entomologist who bought them to study the bats – they rush out at sunset. *No regular opening hours. Admission free, but guides charge a fee.*

Untamed Cockpit Country

Maroons

When the English seized the island in 1655, the Spanish fled, and their slaves, free at last, took to the mountains, where they evolved their own culture. For a century-and-a-half these Maroons (derived from the Spanish *cimarones* from 'cima' meaning peak, as both runaway animals and escaping slaves headed for the mountains) proved a thorn in the side of the English.

The Leeward Maroons lived in the Cockpit Country; the Windward Maroons occupied the Blue Mountains. Led by an Ashanti chief named Cudjoe, the Leewards launched a war against the British that was to last many decades (1690–1739). The Windwards joined them, led by a priestess named Nanny.

Using ruthless guerrilla tactics and assisted by the formidable terrain (Cockpit Country became known as the 'Land of Look Behind' because English soldiers moved back-to-back to avoid ambush), the Maroons harassed the English until the latter gave up. In 1739, the British signed a peace treaty that granted the Leeward Maroons legal autonomy. In exchange, the Maroons agreed to cease their hostilities and to refuse sanctuary to runaway slaves. They also agreed to assist the British in suppressing future slave rebellions.

A Second Maroon War erupted in 1795 when two runaway slaves whom the Maroons had handed over to the English authorities were used to flog two Maroons sentenced for stealing pigs. The five-month war that ensued engulfed the island. Dogs and Indian trackers were eventually imported to track the Maroons, who surrendered. Eventually, 600 Maroons were deported to Sierra Leone, becoming the first New World Africans to be repatriated to Africa.

Today, little remains of Maroon culture. A Maroon Village can be visited; contact the local Jamaica Tourist Board for more information.

Local guides show tourists the Maroon trails

Columbus Park

Columbus Park, 1.5km (1 mile) west of Discovery Bay, marks the site where the famous explorer supposedly first set foot on Jamaica in 1494. The park, an open-air museum, enjoys a superb bluff-top setting overlooking the white-sand-fringed Discovery Bay.

The museum has various historical memorabilia – anchors, cannons, nautical bells, an old water wheel in (albeit creaky) working condition, sugar-boiling 'coppers' and a diminutive locomotive with a 20hp diesel engine that hauled sugar cane at Innswood Estate until 1969. There is also a beautiful mural depicting Columbus's landing.

The town of Discovery Bay is dominated by a bauxite-loading port – Port Rhoades – just west of town. Behind, atop the hill, is a lookout point with superb views.

1.5km (1 mile) west of Discovery Bay. Open: daily 9am–5pm. Free admission.

Cranbrook Flower Forest

Cranbrook is a wonderfully peaceful nature park with landscaped gardens, grassy lawns and a fine collection of orchids. Ghetto blasters are not allowed – perhaps a blessing in noisy Jamaica – and a fast-flowing river runs through the site. You can climb up to the river head where there is a deep pool, perfect for bathing and cooling off. There's a gift shop and snack counter, though most visitors bring their own picnic. The latest addition to the park is a canopy tour which whizzes you through the tree tops on a series of cables.
29km (18 miles) west of Ocho Rios. Tel: (876) 770 8071; www.cranbrookff.com. Open: daily 9am–5pm. Admission charge.

Edinburgh Castle

Some 5km (3 miles) south of Bonneville on the road from Claremont, at Pedro, is the hilltop ruin of Edinburgh Castle. Two loopholed walls and circular towers are all that remain of the once macabre site where a sadistic Scot named Lewis Hutchinson murdered more than 40 innocent passers-by in cold blood in the 1760s.

He is reputed to have decapitated his victims and tossed them into a sinkhole, but no bodies were ever found. The madman was caught while escaping to sea, and hanged.

Falmouth

Ramshackle maybe, but still the best-preserved Georgian town in Jamaica, and well worth two hours' ambling. The bustling activity on Saturday is a reminder of the days when the town grew wealthy trading in sugar, slaves and rum.

The town's 'Bend Down' Wednesday market (because its wares are laid out on the ground) is popular with locals who pour into the town from the hills around and is a typical slice of Jamaican country life.

Traces of Falmouth's former elegance are concentrated along Market Street, west of Water Square. The street was used in the filming of *Papillon*. Many houses have Regency-style, wrought-iron balconies and a projecting upper storey supported on columns to form a piazza at street level.

Points of interest include the Palladian courthouse (a replica of the original building dating back to 1817); the Methodist manse; the cut-stone warehouses of Hampden Wharf; the Phoenix foundry, one of the earliest industrial buildings in Jamaica; and the parish church, built in 1796. The William Knibb Memorial Church, at the corner of George and King streets, commemorates the local Baptist minister whose work was fundamental in the abolition of slavery.

Seaboard Street is still a place to watch the local fishermen bring in their nets. *37km (23 miles) east of Montego Bay.*

Falmouth Swamp Safari

A crocodile farm where James Bond had a scare in *Live and Let Die*. There is a bird sanctuary and petting zoo, and those with the nerve can handle live snakes. *3.5km (2 miles) west of Falmouth. Tel: (876) 974 2870. Open: daily 9am–5pm. Admission charge.*

Firefly

The priceless panorama did not inspire the song 'A Room with a View' – the song was composed in Hawaii in 1928 – but the vistas from Firefly, Sir Noël Coward's holiday retreat, are allegedly 'the finest in the Caribbean'. The house,

built atop a high promontory above Port Maria, is now a museum that looks as it did when the great playwright and novelist died here in 1973.

Coward discovered the site while holidaying with a friend in 1948. Driving around one day, they arrived at a wide plateau where they settled down to paint until dusk, when huge luminous fireflies – locally called *peeny-wallies* or *winkies* – appeared. Coward immediately bought the property and eight years later moved into the beloved home he built there.

Sean Connery, Laurence Olivier and Vivien Leigh, Roald Dahl and Patricia Neal, John Gielgud, David Niven, Peter Sellers and other stars of screen and theatre were all regular guests. Friends would say: 'These Martinis are very strong!' Coward would reply: 'No, no! It's the altitude.'

Coward lies buried beneath a white marble slab. The spot where he sat with

The spectacular view from Firefly

so many illustrious friends, drink in hand, watching the sunset reflect on the sea, is marked by a statue of a man, looking out over the panorama.

Firefly was given to the Jamaica National Heritage Trust in 1976. Today it is administered by Island Outpost on behalf of the Trust. The house has been restored to look as it did on Sunday, 28 February 1965, the day the (now late) Queen Mother came to lunch. Coward's brightly coloured paintings are displayed in his studio; the former garage has been turned into a screening room with a spellbinding video of Coward's life. Within, the simply-furnished house looks like a set from one of his plays, with his two pianos back-to-back in the music room. Upstairs is Coward's so-called room with a view, open on one side, and his bedroom containing his Jamaican pineapple four-poster and a closet full of Hawaiian shirts and silk pyjamas.

The stone hut that was, until recently, a pub was once a lookout post for

lieutenant governor of Jamaica, Henry Morgan.

Fireflies still prance at nightfall.
PO Box 38, Port Maria, St Mary. 3.5km (2 miles) south of Port Maria. Tel: (876) 725 0920; www.islandjamaica.com Open: 9am–5pm. Admission charge.

Green Grotto and Runaway Caves
The unassuming entrance to Runaway Caves gives no hint of the scale and grandeur of the mysterious subterranean world within. A 45-minute tour is highlighted by a boat ride on the eerie, underground Green Grotto Lake where the stalactites are reflected in crystal-clear water some 50m (160ft) beneath the surface. Twenty species of bats, five of which are endemic, inhabit the caves.

Your guide may make the formations chime by striking them with a stick. Spanish troops were thought to have hidden here before fleeing to Cuba in 1655, as well as 18th-century slaves.
3km (2 miles) west of Runaway Bay. Tours run hourly, 9am–5pm. Admission charge.

Good Hope
Ten kilometres (6 miles) south of Falmouth is an unpretentious Georgian Great House, surrounded by meadows and well-tended orchards of coconut palms, papaya and ackee. Good Hope was built in 1755 and grew to be the hub of the largest plantation empire in Jamaica (owner John Tharp eventually owned more than 4,000 hectares/10,000

Gracious living at Good Hope, now a luxury hotel

acres and 3,000 slaves). The estate produced sugar until 1904, then fell into disrepair. It was magnificently restored and reborn in 1993 as a luxury private villa, available to rent. Good Hope maintains a stable of horses, and trails lead through the 809-hectare (2,000-acre) working plantation. Non-guests may sign up for horse-riding tours.

The house has many Palladian details and Adam friezes, plus a beautiful formal entrance with double staircase and columned portico. Among the other well-preserved 18th-century structures are the Slave Hospital and the Counting House, plus parts of the aqueduct and sugar mill with water wheel.
PO Box 50, Falmouth, Trelawny. Tel/fax: (876) 610 5798; www.goodhopejamaica.com

Harmony Hall

Harmony Hall, a large Victorian manor with a green shingle roof and fretwork arches, 6.5km (4 miles) east of Ocho Rios, was built as a Methodist manse with an adjoining pimento estate. Today it is a showcase for the best of Jamaican arts and crafts. The Back Gallery displays works by many of Jamaica's most illustrious artists; the Intuitive Room displays 'Primitive', 'Naïve' and 'Folk' art. Special exhibitions are mounted in the Front Gallery from mid-November to Easter. Its Easter and Christmas fairs are social highlights.
PO Box 192, Ocho Rios. On the coast road, 6.5km (4 miles) east of Ocho Rios. Tel: (876) 975 4222;
www.harmonyhall.com. Open: daily (except Mon) 10am–6pm. Free admission.

Luminous Lagoon

Agitate the waters at Rock, 3.5km (2 miles) east of Falmouth, and they seem to explode. The bay, also known as Luminous Lagoon, contains one of the world's largest concentrations of bioluminescent microorganisms. These tiny creatures light up and glow ghostly green when disturbed. Fish swimming by shine eerily. Past development almost destroyed the phosphorescence, but today it is making a comeback.

Boats can be hired at the jetties behind Glistening Waters and Rose's-by-the-Sea.

Martha Brae River

This river rises from a subterranean chamber in the Cockpit Country and flows south to emerge on the coast at Falmouth. It is popular for bamboo raft trips that begin at Rafter's Village, 3.5km (2 miles) south of town, where friendly Rastafarians will vie to pole you downriver.

Oracabessa

Oracabessa is a sleepy, erstwhile banana port where dugout canoes still pull up on the beach. The village, on the A3, 21km (13 miles) east of Ocho Rios, is more famous as a film setting for *Dr No*, the first of the James Bond films – appropriately, as novelist Ian Fleming

Birds of Jamaica

Jamaica has 252 species of birds, 26 of them indigenous. Their songs and gay plumage brighten every tourist's day.

The national bird – the red-billed streamertail humming bird, or 'doctor bird' – ranges from sea level to Blue Mountain Peak. The male's vivid, shimmering green-blue livery and scissor-shaped, sweeping tail appear everywhere… even on the Jamaican dollar bill and as the logo of Air Jamaica. 'Doctor bird'? Apparently the streamertail's long, needle-like beak resembles the lancets of doctors of old.

Doctor bird

Jamaican Oriole

during his sermons that his face and neck turned red above his black collar.

Two species of parrots, the flamboyant green-back and the yellow-billed, screech and chatter from their perches high in the lowland forest. There are bright-coloured parakeets and finches, too.

The montane forests are filled with the mournful cries of the rufus-throated solitaire and the harsh cries of the red-headed Jamaican woodpecker. The plaintive call of the patoo (the screech or white owl) supposedly signals impending bad luck.

Flycatchers abound, including the loggerhead kingbird, whose black head bears a concealed yellow crown that can be raised when angry. More beautiful still is the indigenous wren-sized Jamaican tody, also known as robin redbreast or Rasta bird. It makes its nest underground. Also common are the Grassquit and the Saffron finch.

Of the sea birds, terns and booby birds return seasonally to nest on outlying coral cays. Pelicans, too, are commonly seen, while frigate birds, with their hooked beaks and sinister forked tails, are easily seen soaring like kites on invisible strings.

Rocklands Bird Feeding Station (*see p110*) is an excellent place to get face to face with Jamaica's most notable birds.

Smallest of Jamaica's four humming bird species is the tiny vervain or bee humming bird; the brightest is the iridescent, rainbow-hued mango humming bird.

A familiar bird is the kling kling, or shiny-black, pearly eyed Antillean grackle, a kleptomaniac that scavenges food from restaurant tables. The wrinkled, bald, bright-red head of the John Crow, too, is seen everywhere. According to local lore, this buzzard is named after the Reverend John Crow, who would spread his black gown like the wings of a bird and become so impassioned conjured up the ace of spies while wintering here.

The origin of Oracabessa is obscure. Some say the name is derived from an Arawak Indian word, *juracabes*. Others say Columbus named the place because of the glow of the sun's rays on the headland – from *oro* (gold) and *cabeza* (head).

Just west of the town is James Bond Beach, a private beach club whose expansive lawns often play host to ear-splitting sound-system parties. A community of stingrays lives offshore and it's possible to take a guided snorkel tour. The club is owned by local-boy-made-good Chris Blackwell whose Island Outpost hotel chain also owns Goldeneye (*see below*).
James Bond Beach Club. Tel: (876) 975 3399; www.islandoutpost.com. Open: Tue–Sat 9am–6pm. Admission charge.

St Mary's Church in Port Maria

Goldeneye

Fleming wintered at his villa, Goldeneye, between 1946 and 1964. He wrote all 13 Bond novels here, naming his hero after the author of the ornithological classic, *Birds of the West Indies*. Graham Greene, Truman Capote, Evelyn Waugh and Fleming's neighbour, Sir Noël Coward, were all frequent guests. The house has gateposts topped by bronze pineapples. Within, it contains much 007 memorabilia. Fleming's house is part of the Goldeneye Estate, a luxury hotel complex with several elegant villas dotted through the grounds and a private beach accessible only by boat (*tel: (876) 975 3354; www.islandoutpost.com*).

Port Maria

About 34km (21 miles) east of Ocho Rios, the A3 sweeps around Galina Point to unveil a majestic, jade-coloured bay, stupendously framed by mountains, with Blue Mountain Peak rising behind. Port Maria stretches along the bayfront.

This small and shabby town, much decayed since its heyday as a thriving banana port, awaits the tourism development that has so far passed it by, despite the beautiful setting.

Of interest, however, is **St Mary's Parish Church** at the west end of town, built of stone in 1861, with a churchyard shaded by palms. The ruin across the street is the former police station, destroyed by fire in 1988. Stop, too, at the 1820 courthouse, where you will find the **Tacky Monument**, which commemorates the leader of the Easter Slave Rebellion of 1760, which began at the Frontier Estate, east of town.

Before leaving, take time to relax on **Pagee Beach**, where you can swim safely and even play dominoes with the local fishermen who may be persuaded to take you out to **Cabarita Island**.

Prospect Plantation

Prospect Plantation, 5km (3 miles) east of Ocho Rios, is a working plantation, redolent with tropical fruits. A covered-jitney ride (and horse-riding trails for the more active) winds past groves of coffee, cacao, citrus, banana and pimento, the aromatic allspice used in Jamaican seasoning. Only pimento and lime are grown commercially; the rest are for show.

Many famous world figures have planted commemorative trees, including Sir Winston Churchill, dramatist Sir Noël Coward, comedian Sir Charles Chaplin and the Duke of Edinburgh.

A guided tour includes a peek inside the chapel of Prospect College, a magnificent stone structure with an old timbered roof. The college prepares boys to enter the defence and police forces. The striking 18th-century Great House (fortified with loopholes against raids by pirates) is now available to rent as a luxury holiday villa (*tel: (876) 994 1508; www.prospect-villas.com*).

Tel: (876) 974 2058. Tours: Mon–Sat 10.30am, 2pm & 3pm; Sun 11am, 1.30pm & 3pm. Horse rides are offered.

Rio Bueno

Most historians agree that this pretty, horseshoe-shaped bay at the mouth of the Rio Bueno is where, having been chased from St Ann's Bay by hostile Indians, Christopher Columbus first landed in Jamaica in 1494. Today, an unspoiled fishing village marks the spot. Decrepit old stone homes and warehouses line the main street, used as a setting for the film *A High Wind in Jamaica*.

St Mark's Anglican Church is pleasingly photogenic, sitting at the water's edge within a walled churchyard, its gateway overgrown with oleander and frangipani.
25km (16 miles) east of Falmouth.

Rio Nuevo

This site, 11km (7 miles) east of Ocho Rios, marks the spot where the Spanish governor, Don Cristobal Ysassi, was defeated by Oliver Cromwell's soldiers in June 1658.

You would never guess the site's historical importance but for the marker that reads: 'On this ground on June 17, 1658, was fought the battle of Rio Nuevo to decide whether Jamaica would be Spanish or English. On one side were the Jamaicans of both black and white races, whose ancestors had come to Jamaica from Africa and Spain 150 years before. On the other side were the English invaders. The Spanish forces lost the battle and the island. The Spanish whites fled to Cuba but the black population took to the mountains and fought a long and bloody guerrilla war against the English. This site is dedicated to all of them.'

Another memorial stands at the site of the old Spanish stockade near the mouth of the river. Sit awhile on the benches under shady pimento (allspice) trees and take in the fine view.

Runaway Bay

Runaway Bay is touted as the place where Spanish forces fled Jamaica for Cuba after the decisive battle with the British in 1658. The name is more probably derived from the traffic in runaway slaves, who were harboured by illegal Spanish traders using this area for runs to Cuba.

Today, escapees arrive here for sunning, diving and golf. The town is virtually nonexistent, though there are several all-inclusive hotels and many villas, plus a superb golf course that is the site of Jamaica's oldest golf tournament, the annual Jamaica Pro-Am, held each November.
27km (17 miles) west of Ocho Rios.

St Ann's Bay

At this site explorer Christopher Columbus first arrived at Jamaica on 5 May 1494. He named the bay Santa Gloria, 'on account of the extreme beauty of its country', before sailing away. A bronze figure of the explorer, on the A3 west of town, is inscribed with images of Columbus's three caravels. It was cast in his native city, Genoa.

The town is more famous, however, as the birthplace of national hero **Marcus Garvey**, born 17 August 1887. A larger-than-life statue of Garvey, considered the father of black nationalism in Jamaica, stands outside the St Ann's Parish Library.

In 1919, Garvey moved to the USA, having founded the Universal Negro Improvement Association (UNIA). His calls for self-reliance stirred black consciousness. He launched a steamship company, the Black Star Line, to repatriate blacks to Africa. The white establishment gaoled him on false charges, destroying his movement. Garvey died in London in 1940.

St Ann's Baptist Church, founded in 1827, faces an old, tumbledown market topped by a pretty wooden clock tower. The 1866 courthouse, on the main street next to the parish church, is interesting for its pedimented porch. To the east is the old English fort, built of stone blocks hauled from Sevilla Nueva.

St Ann's prettiest structure is **Our Lady of Perpetual Help Church**, at the west end of the town. This little gem is of Spanish design and festooned with climbing plants. Palms lead through beautifully landscaped grounds.
11km (7 miles) west of Ocho Rios.

Sevilla Nueva

One kilometre ($^1/_2$ mile) west of St Ann's Bay, the A3 runs through Sevilla

Nueva, the first Spanish settlement in Jamaica.

On his fourth and last voyage to the New World in 1503, Columbus careened his two worm-eaten vessels, *Capitana* and *Santiago de Palos*, at this site. (The ships are believed to lie offshore.) Abandoned by the Spanish governor in Hispaniola, Columbus spent a year and four days stranded in St Ann's Bay.

A dirt road on the seaward side leads to the Columbus site, where a sign reads: 'The first known Jamaicans, the Arawaks, encountered Columbus and the Spaniards on this property.'

In November 1509, Don Juan de Esquivel, who had been with Columbus in 1494, returned and laid the foundations of Sevilla Nueva. The town, which included a fortress, church, and the first sugar mill in Jamaica, never prospered – it was built too close to the swamps. After 24 years the capital was transferred to Villa de la Vega, today's Spanish Town. Crumbling stone structures are all that remain of the early Spanish habitation (artefacts found here are now in the Institute of Jamaica). In 1645, Richard Hemming, an officer in the Cromwellian army, despoiled the Spanish ruins to build the Sevilla Estate on the landward side of the highway. A road leads to the 'busha' (overseer's) house, sugar mill, copra kiln, water wheel and boiling house that make up the 'English Industrial Works', part of **Seville Great House and Heritage Park**. Seville Great House sits on the ridge above, with a commanding view over Sevilla Nueva. Today, the site is operated as a museum by the National Heritage Trust. A video tells the history of the site.

1km (^{1}/$_2$ mile) west of St Ann's Bay. Tel: (876) 972 2191; www.jnht.com. Open: daily 9am–5pm. Admission charge for the museum & Great House.

White River

This small river, 3km (2 miles) east of Ocho Rios, is a popular rafting spot. Fishing boats and rafts gather at the river mouth where there are several restaurants. Not far from here and well signposted is the White River Valley Park. No expense has been spared in developing this lush pastoral landscape into an activity centre, with horse riding, tubing and kayaking.

White River Valley Park. Tel: (876) 917 3373; www.wrvja.com. Open: daily 8am–6pm. Admission charge.

A Runaway Bay shopkeeper is pleased to offer conch shells and woodcarvings for sale

The west

The west is neatly demarcated by the parishes of St James, Hanover and Westmoreland. Together they offer virtually everything the visitor to Jamaica hopes for. Montego Bay is the first place most visitors to Jamaica see. It offers a pretty fair sampling of what the island has to offer: stunning beaches, hotels of every description, lots of golf, tennis and water sports, river rafting, intriguing history including a working plantation and several Great Houses, plus good nightlife, restaurants and shopping.

The young-at-heart, regardless of age, head for Negril. This one-time haven for pirates and passing whalers and, later, for hippies, is today a town of simple pleasures. It is as laid-back or as lively as you wish.

There's mo'fun, mo'sun and mo'to do in Mo'Bay! Montego Bay, or 'Mo'Bay' as locals call it, is Jamaica's biggest resort, with activities to suit every taste. Most of the options are based on the beach or on, over or under the crystalline waters of the recently created Montego Bay Marine Park, a 2,400-hectare

(6,000-acre) marine reserve that captivates water enthusiasts. Broader pleasures await within a short drive of town. A bevy of plantation homes awaits exploration. Most well known is Rose Hall, an 18th-century mansion that is said to be haunted by the wicked White Witch. Worth a look, too, is Croydon, a working plantation. A short jaunt into the hills also leads to a bird feeding station, the German settlement of Seaford Town, and Frome and the sugar estates of the Westmoreland Plain. Speaking of sugar, do not miss a sojourn at the Appleton Rum Estate.

You can head off on your own along back roads that will give you a taste of the real Jamaica. Take your camera – the scenery is spectacular. Should you choose to explore *terra incognita* on foot, take a guide – the back country is a patchwork of illegal *ganja* (marijuana) plots. It is not a good idea to trespass!

Montego Bay's Doctor's Cave Beach demonstrates the delights that the west has to offer

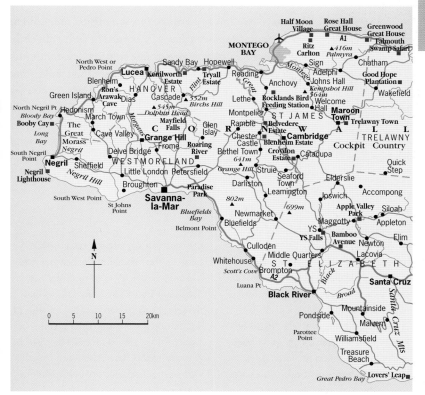

Nowhere better epitomises Jamaica's '*No problem, mon!*' attitude than Negril, at the westernmost tip of the island. It is difficult not to fall right into its shrug-off-the-blues way of life. The beach seems endless. The calm waters are a palette of light blues and greens. And the consistently spectacular sunsets get more applause than the live reggae concerts for which Negril is famous.

Being so popular, the region caters to many tastes. Accommodation ranges from sophisticated, all-inclusive resorts

to budget cottages and quaint bed-and-breakfast inns. Tryall, the Ritz-Carlton and Half Moon deserve singling out as 'elegant resorts', with their own championship golf courses that are among the most beautiful and challenging in the Caribbean.

Getting around is easy. Both Negril and Mo'Bay have a surfeit of scooters and motorbikes for hire. Rental cars are generally easily come by (do book ahead), and day excursions are widely available.

Montego Bay

Montego Bay lures sun worshippers with its magnificent setting: an aquamarine bay surrounded by lush green hills and fringed by soft white sands. Jamaica's holiday hub flows over with things to do and places to see. Like other tourist centres, however, Mo'Bay has bad mixed in with the good. Its street vendors, for example, are notoriously pushy. Fortunately, the Jamaica Tourist Board is making far-reaching efforts, and attempts to allay this problem have been largely successful. The following information will better acquaint you with whether Mo'Bay is for you.

Christopher Columbus dropped anchor here in 1494. Jamaica's first visitor named the bay The Gulf of Good Weather. No one disputes it. The town's start, however, was more ignominious – as the lard capital of the Caribbean. 'Montego' derives from the Spanish word for hog fat, *manteca*. Wild boars in the hills supplied the lard. Later, it became a major port for bananas and sugar. Many of the magnificent homes of the sugar barons remain.

Mo'Bay sprang to life as a spa resort in the early 1900s. The supposedly beneficial sea waters – and the beaches – are what started it all, especially Doctor's Cave Beach, where tourists and locals alike head on a typically beautiful day. Very few come today for a Doctor's Cave treatment, though everybody finds Mo'Bay just what the doctor ordered.

There are really two Montego Bays: the town centre and the touristy hotel strip along Gloucester Avenue, north of the centre. It is a twenty-minute walk between the two. Sadly, the beaches are hidden from view for most of the way. What you would like to see lies beyond fencing. En route you pass the remains of Fort Montego, as dishevelled as the wasteland backing Walter Fletcher Beach. A crafts market here brims with bargains, as does the larger one at Howard Cooke Boulevard and Strand Street.

Downtown is a hive of activity. St James Street is the main thoroughfare. At its core is Sam Sharpe Square, which evokes sombre memories. Church Street is well worth a stroll for its cluster of historic buildings, including St James Parish Church. Fustic Market, on Barnett Street, is a whirligig of colour and noise where the people of Mo'Bay do their shopping and gossiping. Close by is Jarrett Park, Montego Bay's cricket ground where Bob Marley and the Wailers once

Montego Bay

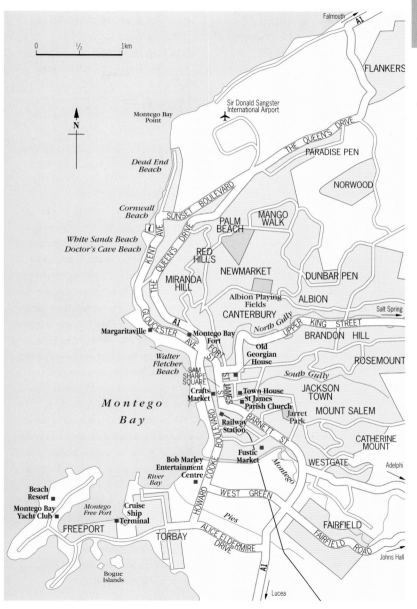

played. Watching a match here is great fun, with booming music and impassioned fans.

Mo'Bay has Mo'Rooms – 40 per cent of all hotel rooms in Jamaica! – and restaurants that run the gamut from poor to superb. Take your pick from a string of options along Gloucester Avenue or head further west out of town for some of the city's finest dining. Additionally, several excellent restaurants are associated wth the all-inclusive hotels in nearby Ironshore.

Mo'Bay's nightlife is split between touristy Gloucester Avenue, which has several all-night discos, and the wilder local clubs of downtown. On Monday nights a street dance is held on Barnett Street – be warned that, although perfectly safe, it's a very Jamaican event.

The Jamaica Tourist Board office (tel: (876) 952 4425; www.visitjamaica.com) is at Cornwall Beach. JTB information desks are also located at the airport and next to the public library at Fort St and Howard Cooke Blvd. Montego Bay has its own comprehensive website: www.montego-bay-jamaica.com

Beaches

Montego Bay's handful of beaches all share the same transparent waters and shimmering white sands. Several resorts pivot on their own private beaches. The public beaches are concentrated in the heart of the tourist strip, along Gloucester Avenue. Coral reefs grow just offshore and are easily seen by snorkellers or glass-bottomed boat. Water sports are widely available.

Dead End Beach

This is Mo'Bay's only decent public beach, a narrow strip of sand right by the airport. Planes fly perilously close overhead but the water is clear and there are often friendly Jamaican families bathing and vendors selling snacks and cold drinks.

Doctor's Cave Beach

Beloved by repeat visitors to Mo'Bay, this arc of sugar-white coral sand is credited with providing the genesis of Jamaica's tourist trade. It was once the property of an eccentric physician, Dr Alexander McCatty, who donated the beach to the city as a bathing club in 1906. A few years later, an enterprising British physician popularised the sea waters here for their supposed curative powers, attracting tourists and a nucleus of small hotels which rose behind the beach.

Today it is a thriving tourist area, equipped with all facilities, including changing rooms, water-sports options and even a pier from which leaves a glass-bottomed boat excursion. The Groovy Grouper restaurant and bar is particularly popular at sundown.
Opposite the Gloucestershire Hotel. Tel: (876) 952 2566; www.doctorscavebathingclub.com. Open: daily 9am–5pm. Admission charge.

Walter Fletcher Beach

Another public beach between the town centre and the hotel enclave on Gloucester Avenue. It is named after a former Custos (*see p14*) of St James. You pass through an unwelcoming and unkempt lawn which locals tend to use as a rubbish dump, but the beach is clean and the water sports facilities here are the most comprehensive in Montego Bay. There are changing rooms, a restaurant and a popular go-kart track. The beach often hosts live music and sound-system events.

Tel: (876) 979 9447;
www.aquasoljamaica.com

Margaritaville

More of an event than a bar, Margaritaville is Montego Bay's biggest tourist attraction. Downstairs there is a gift shop, a team of all-singing, all-dancing barmen and an extensive list of tequila- and rum-based cocktails. The roof is even more exciting, with a Jacuzzi, sun decks and a 30m (100ft) water slide which runs right down to the sea below.

Gloucester Avenue. Tel: (876) 952 4777;
www.margaritavillecaribbean.com

Montego Bay Fort

Virtually nothing remains of the bastion built in 1752 to protect Montego Bay. Three large brass cannons, green with patina, still point out to sea. They were fired only twice: in 1760 to celebrate the capture of Havana when, alas, one blew up and killed the cannoneer; and in 1795, when the cannons were loosed at a British ship, the *Mercury*, which sailed in at dusk and was mistaken for a French privateer.

The fort is bisected by Fort Street. A crafts market occupies the leeward side of it.

Open: all day daily. Free admission.

So perfect was Doctor's Cave Beach that it made Jamaica famous as a tourist getaway

St James Parish Church

St James Parish Church, built between 1775 and 1782, is regarded as one of the finest churches in Jamaica. The venerable building was constructed of limestone in the shape of a Greek cross. Note the deep cracks – a legacy of the devastating earthquake of 1 March 1957 (the church was extensively damaged, and rebuilt in 1958). Within are several marble monuments erected by the early sugar barons. One, by the famous English sculptor John Bacon (1740–99), is dedicated to Rose Palmer, the virtuous wife maligned in legend as the White Witch of Rose Hall (*see pp108–9*).

The palm-shaded churchyard contains graves dating back 200 years. Most are delapidated, and some are so weathered as to be barely legible.

Sam Sharpe Square

Despite the island's seductive appeal, it is difficult to avoid her less savoury history. Sam Sharpe Square, in the centre of town, brims with memories of the slave trade.

The square is named after local Baptist minister 'Daddy' Sam Sharpe who led the Christmas Slave Rebellion of 1831. The British authorities reacted by hanging Sharpe in the square. He and 500 followers were strung four at a time on the gibbet.

When laid out in 1755 it was called The Parade, and, later, Charles Square in honour of the then governor, Admiral Charles Knowles. Its centrepiece is a pretty bronze fountain (painted silver) on a roundabout; it functions intermittently, and is dedicated to John Edward Kerr (1840–1903), who pioneered the local banana trade. Note the drinking troughs placed at varied heights to quench the thirst of man, horse and dog.

The southwest corner of the square is dominated by the lavishly rebuilt Montego Bay Civic Centre. The Georgian-style building replaces the old Courthouse which was burnt down in 1968. It now houses a performing arts space and a small museum of local history.

Tel: (876) 952 5500; www.stjamespc.org. Open: Tue–Fri 9am–5pm, Sat 10am–3pm, Sun noon–5pm. Admission charge for museum.

The bustling square was spruced up in the mid-1980s and lavishly paved in stone. It is a gathering place for locals and a good place to sit and watch Jamaicans at work and play. You may chance upon a lively debate during periods of election fever, when the square is a centre of political action.

Note the restored period structures occupied by Jamaica's leading banks.

The Cage

The tiny antique building on the northwest corner dates back to 1806. Bars on the windows speak of its history as a gaol for 'runaway' slaves and any blacks who were found on the streets after 3pm on Sundays. The tiny steeple contains a bell, rung at 2pm during slave days to warn blacks that the curfew would soon begin. The Cage has since found many uses, and at the time of writing houses a craft shop.

Sam Sharpe Memorial

Fronting The Cage is an impressive bronze statue of national heroes Paul Bogle and Sam Sharpe, the latter with Bible in hand, addressing a rapt audience. The tableau of five bronze statues was unveiled in 1984.

Town House

This elegant Georgian town house is made of red brick brought as ballast from England. It was built in 1765 by a wealthy merchant, David Morgan. It later served as the church manse, the house of a Jamaican governor's mistress, a Masonic lodge, and finally a hotel, when it occasioned a husband–lover confrontation, the legacy of which is a bullet hole in the mahogany staircase.

The house – now a law office – is festooned with rambling laburnum that climbs to the roof.
16 Church St. Tel: (876) 952 2660.

Accompong

Accompong is the capital of the western Maroons, the recalcitrant society of escaped slaves and their descendants. It is a forbidding drive along deep-rutted, narrow roads that lead into the edge of the Cockpit Country.

The hamlet, 13km (8 miles) north of Maggotty, is little more than a string of shacks and small houses along the roadside. The Presbyterian Church is the sole structure of substance. A National Trust monument at the crossroads commemorates Cudjoe, the Maroon leader who held the British

Sam Sharpe Square is quiet now but has seen troubled times in the past

Mangroves reach into the water

Army at bay before signing the 1739 peace treaty that ratified the settlement at Accompong and ceded 405 hectares (1,000 acres) to the Maroons.

Accompong is named after Cudjoe's brother. It is surrounded by scenery so marvellous that it is difficult to imagine that the area has such bitter memories.

The township still operates semi-autonomously under a town council headed by a 'Colonel' elected by ballot (for many years the Jamaican government had no jurisdiction over the Maroons, except where the crime was murder). It is still considered respectful to pay a call on the Colonel. Locals may attempt to extract an entrance fee to the village.

On Treaty Day (6 January) the drums begin to beat, abeng horns trumpet loudly, animals are slaughtered for traditional feasts, and people flock from far and wide for the ensuing celebration.

Appleton Rum Estate

You do not have to like rum to enjoy a visit to Jamaica's oldest and largest rum factory – the heart of a 4,400-hectare (10,800-acre) plantation that nestles in the breathtakingly beautiful valley of the Black River. A tour of the distillery reveals the process by which J Wray and Nephew Ltd have been producing superb rums since 1749. King George III and George Washington apparently considered Appleton rums 'the rum of choice'. Some of the copper distillation pots that are still in use date back over a century.

Dozens of tour operators run trips to Appleton (*see Directory, Organised tours, page 186*). Independent holidaymakers are also welcome. There is a hospitality lounge, plus gift shop, coffee shop, restaurant (advance orders only) and bar. *Jamaica Estate Tours, c/o Appleton Estate, Siloah, St Elizabeth. On the B6, 3km (2 miles) west of Siloah. Tel: (876) 963 9215; www.appletonrum.com. Open: Mon–Sat 9am–4pm, last tour is at 3.30pm. Admission charge.*

Black River

Black River, capital of St Elizabeth, is the gateway to the south coast. It is one of Jamaica's most peaceful towns, strung along a jade-blue bay. Gingerbread houses enhance the general charm of the High Street, where old-style colonnaded timber houses lead to the dock at the river mouth. The river is stained dark as molasses by minerals.

Marvel at the view from the bridge at the river mouth, where fishing trawlers gather and ships are still loaded by lighters, as they were in the 19th century when a boom in the logwood trade brought brief prosperity.

Two architectural highlights are the porticoed courthouse and yellow-brick church that face the water. The timber-framed Waterloo Guest House was the first building in Jamaica to install electric lighting, in 1893.
69km (43 miles) west of Mandeville, 50km (31 miles) southeast of Savanna-la-Mar.

Blenheim

You could buzz through Blenheim with no hint that this hamlet was the birthplace of the Rt Excellent Sir Alexander Bustamante.

Perhaps the most colourful of Jamaica's many colourful political figures, Bustamante entered politics at the relatively late age of 50 and worked assiduously on behalf of the poor and underprivileged. He founded the Jamaica Labour Party before becoming Jamaica's first prime minister in 1962.

His father, Robert Clarke, was an overseer on the Blenheim Estate. The modest shack in which Bustamante was raised is now a small museum with interesting displays on his life and times. *Tel: (876) 326 8138; www.jnht.com. Open: daily 9am–5pm. Admission charge.*

A memorial service is held here annually on 6 August – the anniversary of Bustamante's death.
5km (3 miles) east of Davis Cove, 10km (6 miles) southwest of Lucea.

Bluefields Bay

The beautiful sweep of Bluefields Bay, east of Savanna-la-Mar, has long been popular – today with locals and the occasional tourist enamoured of its wide, gently curving beach, in times gone by with pirates who favoured its

Waterloo Guest House, Black River

A lookout point in Bluefields Bay

good anchorage. Henry Morgan set sail from here in 1670 on his infamous raid on Panama. At **Belmont Point**, at the south end of the bay, is a fort built in 1767 by an estate owner as protection against pirates.

The shore is lined with jerk stands, and coconut vendors stalk the beach, which gets crowded at weekends and during holidays.

These are prime fishing waters, good for spiny lobsters and gamefish such as tuna, bonito and sailfish. You may still see local fishermen in canoes hewn from cotton trees.

17.5km (11 miles) east of Savanna-la-Mar, 32km (20 miles) west of Black River.

Catadupa

The charming railway village of Catadupa nestles on the deeply forested western fringe of the Cockpit Country. Coffee is grown locally and there is a small factory for washing and pulping coffee beans.

The hamlet was once a stop for the **Appleton Express** that operated until 1992 between Montego Bay and the Appleton Rum Factory. Many of Catadupa's inhabitants derived much of their income from tailoring shirts and blouses for passengers. Passengers in need of these services were measured on the outbound journey and picked up the finished garment on the return. The tiny railway station still stands.

Catadupa is the Greek name for the Nile cataracts.
30km (18 miles) south of Montego Bay.

Croydon Estate

This 53-hectare (132-acre) plantation on the outskirts of Catadupa grows coffee, pineapples and citrus on steep, terraced hills. A 'see, hear, touch and taste' tour lets you sample tropical fruits in season, and you can watch coffee being processed.

National hero Sam Sharpe was born here. He rose to become a 'daddy' or leader of the native Baptists of Montego Bay, and led the 1831 Slave Rebellion for which he was hanged. Sam Sharpe Square in Montego Bay is so-named in his honour.

Croydon can be visited on a half-day tour from Montego Bay. The tour includes a Jamaican barbecue lunch at a hilltop restaurant that also provides inspirational views.

Tel: (876) 979 8267;
www.croydonplantation.com.
Tours on Tue, Wed & Fri; 10.30am–3pm.
Admission charge.

Elderslie

Elderslie, 13km (8 miles) north of
Maggotty, bills itself as the 'heart of the
Cockpit Country', although it lies on
the fringe. Its inhabitants dubiously
also claim ancestry from the Maroons,
who lived in the Cockpits.

Less controversial is that it is home to
some of Jamaica's leading woodcarvers,
who skilfully handle mallets and chisels
to craft subtle, delicate forms from
blocks of lignum vitae.

While here, also peek inside the
Wondrous Caves, which contain
a small underground lake.
Wondrous Caves are located at Cook
Bottom. Admission free, but local guides
charge a fee.

Frome

Frome is a sugar town set in a 155sq-
km (60sq-mile) alluvial plain that is
one of the two largest sugar-producing
areas in Jamaica. Frome Sugar Factory
was for many years the largest in the
West Indies. It was built in 1938 by the
West Indies Sugar Company to process
the sugar from their 16 estates.

The factory's opening precipitated
violent labour troubles when thousands
of unemployed people migrated to the
region seeking work. At that time, men
received only 15 cents a day for their
labour; women were paid 10 cents.

Labour activist Alexander Bustamante
(*see also p99*) became the champion of
the workers' cause (and later Jamaica's
first prime minister).

A monument in town celebrates
'Labour Leader Bustamante and the
workers for their courageous fight in
1938 on behalf of the working people
of Jamaica'.

Factory visits can be arranged by
prior request (*tel: (876) 955 6080*). A
good time is between November and
June, during the sugar harvest.
8km (5 miles) north of Savanna-la-Mar.

Great River

This moderate-sized river forms the
boundary between St James and
Hanover. It is a popular carriageway for
soothing one-hour rafting trips from
Lethe, a small mountain village with an
old stone bridge built in 1828 and
faithfully restored after it was toppled
by the 1957 earthquake. The 'rapids' are
sufficient to rouse you from reverie,
and it's now possible to enjoy them
properly with a thrilling white-water
rafting tour. (*See pp142–3.*)
Caliche Rafting. Tel: (876) 940 1745;
www.whitewaterraftingmontegobay.com

Fishing enthusiasts may be tempted
to cast for snook and tarpon in the
river mouth, 19km (12 miles) west of
Montego Bay.

Greenwood Great House

Greenwood Great House, 27.5km (17
miles) east of Montego Bay, was built in
the 1790s as a guesthouse by the family

of poet Elizabeth Barrett Browning. The Barretts came to Jamaica in the 1660s and grew immensely wealthy from their sugar estate.

The fieldstone and wood plantation-style home retains its historic ambience. Guides in plantation dress lead tours.

Greenwood is perhaps the finest antique museum in the Caribbean. Its marvels include the original library, with rare books dating from 1697, in addition to a fine collection of oil paintings, Wedgwood china, musical instruments, a court jester's chair, a mantrap (used for catching runaway slaves), and an inlaid rosewood piano given as a betrothal gift by Edward VII to his fianceé. Other items include horse-drawn carriages, a hearse and antique firefighting equipment, which are displayed in the gardens.

The long veranda on the north façade provides a breathtaking panorama of the Caribbean and Barrett's estate.

Greenwood Great House, PO Box 169, Montego Bay. Tel: (876) 953 1077. Open: daily 9am–6pm. Admission charge.

Ipswich Cave

Often inaccurately described as Jamaica's second-largest cave, Ipswich Cave is located 30.5km (19 miles) north of Black River. Nevertheless, the great vaulted chambers are cut deep into the limestone massif called the Cockpit Country, with galleries full of mesmerising formations. Walkways

Neat rows of sugar cane near Frome

lead through the well-lit caves. Local guides are on hand to rent their services.

The site was once a call on the itinerary of the Appleton Express. The railway still passes by, but, alas, trains no longer run.

No set opening hours. Admission free, but local guides charge a fee.

Kenilworth

This erstwhile sugar estate preserves the ruins of one of Jamaica's best examples of 17th-century industrial architecture.

A derelict Great House overlooks the remains of the massively constructed sugar mill and boiling house-cum-distillery. Note the large oval Palladian windows. A further education college now occupies much of the estate.

The tomb of estate owner Thomas Blagrove (1733–55) claims 'his humane treatment of his servants, in a region not abounding in such examples, induced their cheerful obedience'.

8km (5 miles) east of Lucea.

Little London

About 36,400 Indians came to Jamaica as indentured labourers after the abolition of slavery. Some 12,000 settled around Little London. Conditions were hardly any better for the Indians than for the slaves. Mortality was so high that in 1914 the Indian government forbade further migration.

Curry brought from India is today a staple of Jamaican cuisine. The Indians also brought *ganja* (marijuana), now ubiquitous throughout the island.

These days ethnic origins have been blurred and Little London is a sleepy roadside community with a couple of decent Jamaican eateries and a drag-racing track.

11km (7 miles) west of Savanna-la-Mar, straddling a crossroads on the A2.

Lucea

The once-prosperous sugar port is now a somnolent fishing harbour that springs to life only on market days. 'Lucy' shelters on the western shore of a mile-wide harbour.

Despite its shabby appearance, architectural highlights include the 19th-century Georgian courthouse fronted by a fountain in the town square. The stone structure with arched veranda is topped by a wooden second storey. Note the clock tower (built about 1817) supported on pseudo-Corinthian columns and supposedly modelled after the helmet of the German Royal Guard. A single family has had the job of keeping the clock in working fettle for over a century.

In the 19th century, Lucea had many Jewish merchants. Their stores remain on Main Street, along with an old fireproof warehouse with an arched interior and double-barrel roof.

Peek inside the parish church (on the corner of Fort Charlotte Drive and the A1) to peruse monuments to prominent Jamaican personalities. Close by are the remains of **Fort Charlotte**, which guards the harbour. The octagonal fortress retains three massive cannons on rotary carriages. A frigate bird colony nests on the cliff. Fort Charlotte, named after the wife of King George III, still has cannons in place and now houses a school. Next door, the old gaol for recalcitrant slaves houses the **Hanover Museum**, a small but interesting collection of historical artefacts.

45km (28 miles) west of Montego Bay. Tel: (876) 956 2584. Open: Mon–Fri 8.30am–4.30pm.

Maggotty

This sleepy market town stretches along the banks of the Black River. An impressive waterfall, alas, was sacrificed to produce hydroelectric power. A bauxite-processing factory haunts the townscape. Fortunately, it is no longer in use, as it was polluting the river.

Apple Valley Park

On the riverbank in the centre of town is a small nature park with animals, a medicinal herb garden and paddle boats on a pond (*tel: (876) 963 9508*). *30.5km (19 miles) north of Black River.*

Maroon Town

Despite its name, the hamlet of Maroon Town, 26km (16 miles) southeast of Montego Bay, did not remain a settlement of Maroons (escaped slaves and their descendants) for long. The British, tired of attempting to suppress the Maroons, built a series of fortified barracks throughout the region. One such sits atop the former Maroon

Lucea is proud of the unusual clock tower which surmounts its courthouse

settlement of **Trelawny Town**, 2km (1 mile) east of Maroon Town. The remains of the encampment can still be seen.

Mayfield Falls

A series of numerous small waterfalls and swimming holes which run through bamboo glades in the foothills of the Dolphin Head Mountains, Mayfield Falls is one of the loveliest spots in Jamaica. Entrance to the Falls is controlled by two separate tour companies who offer the same exhilarating experience of climbing the river with an experienced guide who points out all the best places to swim, dive or take a natural shower. It really is an isolated place, though, and if you drive yourself you're bound to get lost. You're better off taking a tour with

one of several operators who run trips to the Falls from Negril or Montego Bay.
Tel (876) 953 3034;
www.mayfieldfalls.com.
Tel (876) 957 3444;
www.riverwalkatmayfield.com.
Open: daily 9am–6pm.
Admission charge.

Middle Quarters

Middle Quarters, 'shrimp capital of Jamaica', is a tiny village where women-folk wait to waylay motorists with little pink bags full of the region's speciality – peppered shrimp. Stop to sample, but make sure you choose a vendor close to a bar shack selling very cold Red Stripe beer. The shrimp are drawn from local rivers using traps of split bamboo.
On the A2, 10km (6 miles) north of
Black River.

Negril

Negril is Jamaica's most laid-back resort – a place where virtually anything goes. Forget the sightseeing. Negril is for languorous sunning by day and bacchanalia by night.

Negril's star attraction is its stunning 11km- (7-mile-) long beach that slopes gently into jade-coloured water. The town was cut off from development (or protected, depending on your perspective) by crocodile-infested swamps until 1965, when the road link with Montego Bay, 84km (52 miles) away, was completed.

Negril quickly became a nirvana for those seeking the 'alternative lifestyle'. Some visitors discovered 'magic mushrooms' – hallucinogens – that are still available in raw form or in a local speciality, mushroom tea.

When a resort called Hedonism opened in 1977, tales of an uninhibited lifestyle launched Negril to fame. The mid-1980s saw a burst of hotel development that has not yet ended. Fortunately, a strict building code has kept the resorts from growing taller than the palms that border the beach.

Negril still retains its laid-back roots. Dressing for dinner means popping a

Montego Bay

The shrimp-sellers of Middle Quarters

Just a part of the giant Negril Beach

T-shirt over your swimsuit. By day everyone sunbathes, with breaks for snorkelling, jetskiing or a parasail ride. The evening ritual is to gather, with rum punch in hand, to watch the sun slide from view into a molten sea below a sky of flaming orange and plum purple. After sunset, Negril comes to life with pounding discos and live reggae concerts.

A virtually ruler-straight road, Norman Manley Boulevard, runs the length of Long Bay. North of the tiny town centre, Negril beach is flanked by a non-stop line of all-inclusive resorts. To the south, West End Road meanders past a kaleidoscope of small hotels, restaurants and funky food stalls that offer everything from 'magic mushroom' omelettes to nouvelle cuisine. The entire West End sits atop dramatically sculpted cliffs that loom over the clear waters.

Negril's hustlers can be annoying in their attempt to sell *ganja* (marijuana) in joints the size of bazookas!
The Jamaica Tourist Board office is now closed. Information is available at the TPDCO (Tourist Product Development Company) in Times Square (tel: (876) 957 9314).

The Great Morass
This huge expanse of wetland pushes right up to the beach. Much of the 3km- (2-mile-) wide swamp remains unexplored. It is a refuge for crocodiles, as well as egrets, jacanas and other rare birds. The Negril River, which drains the swamps, is stained dark by peat deposits. Various earlier attempts to drain the swamps washed large amounts of silt out to sea, destroying a portion of the coral reef. Inevitably, there is a fierce ongoing battle between developers and environmentalists.

Bloody Bay

This scalloped bay, north of Long Bay, is the setting for de luxe, all-inclusive resorts. However, where nudists now frolic, whales were once beached and butchered.

The British Royal Navy considered the bay 'conveniently situated for its men-of-war, during any rupture with Spain, to lie in wait for Spanish vessels passing to and fro from Havana'. In 1702, a naval squadron under Admiral Benbow mustered here; another gathered in 1814 before bombarding New Orleans. The pirate 'Calico' Jack Rackham (named for his penchant for calico underwear) was captured here in 1720, after lingering in the company of his amorous but no less bloodthirsty consorts, Anne Bonney and Mary Read. Rackham was strung from the gibbet at Port Royal; the female pirates 'pleaded their stomachs, being quick with child' and were spared execution.

The islet offshore is Booby Cay, famous as a South Sea location in Walt Disney's *20,000 Leagues Under the Sea*. It is a nesting site for booby birds.

Negril Lighthouse

Negril's only historical structure is the lighthouse, which celebrated its centenary in 1994. Located at 18° 15' north by 78° 23' west, it marks the most westerly point of Jamaica, 5km (3 miles) south of the town.

It is possible to climb the 103 stairs by arrangement with the keeper. Among other things of interest are the original kerosene lamps. Today, the 20m- (66ft-) tall lighthouse gives warning with an automatic, solar-powered light.

Paradise Park

A working cattle ranch on the outskirts of Savanna-la-Mar, Paradise Park is also just that – a wonderfully peaceful spot where you can hike, horse-ride, swim in the Sweet River or lounge in grassy meadows. Bring your own picnic as there's no restaurant on site.
Tel: (876) 848 9826. Open: Mon–Sat 8.30am–4.30pm.
Admission charge.

Roaring River Park and Blue Hole Gardens

Roaring River Park is set in a former plantation close to the village of Petersfield and is a pretty landscaped garden alongside a gushing river and a series of impressive caverns which range from tiny to vast in size. Several pools packed with minerals and said to have healing properties are found deep within the cave network. Ten minutes'

Sunset over Negril lights up the sky

The White Witch of Rose Hall

The sordid saga of the White Witch of Rose Hall is more fictional than factual … but it is an exhilarating tale nonetheless!

The legend tells of Annie Palmer, the wicked mistress who ruled over Rose Hall for 13 years. This epic of iniquity begins in 1820, when estate owner John Rose Palmer married his 18-year-old Irish bride, Annie May Patterson. Said to have been trained in voodoo by a Haitian priestess, Rose Hall's new mistress was as sadistic and sinful as she was petite and pretty.

An artist's impression of Annie Palmer on the book cover

She tortured her slaves and lured into bed any man, black or white, whom she fancied.

According to a late Victorian version of the tale, she 'poisoned her first husband, aided by her paramour, a Negro, whom she flogged to death to close his lips; again married, poisoned her second husband, whose death she hastened by stabbing him with a knife; married her second paramour … who disappeared mysteriously …'

Her fourth husband wisely abandoned her, leaving the lascivious Annie to the company of her slaves. Her orgy of dissipation ended one morning in 1833 when a slave lover strangled her in her bed at the Great House.

The tale is apocryphal. It is based on the fact that Annie Palmer, the first mistress of Rose Hall, indeed had four husbands. She died at the age of 72 in the 23rd year of her marriage to John Palmer, founder of Rose Hall. Research proves that the real Annie was also a model wife to John Rose Palmer. She died peacefully at Bonavista near Montego Bay in 1846.

The kernel of the legend arose even while Annie Palmer was still alive. The Reverend Hope Waddell, writing of

Rose Hall (18th century)

the neighbouring Palmer property of Palmyra, recorded having being shown 'the iron collars and spikes used by a lady owner there for the necks of her slaves, and also the bed on which she was found dead one morning, having been strangled'. In 1868 the editor of the Falmouth Post apparently had the notion of linking Waddell's story with memories of a much-married mistress, and published a story in which Annie Palmer first appeared as an evil murderess. The tale is marvellously told in the novel *The White Witch of Rosehall*, written by Herbert G de Lisser in 1958.

The witch is still rumoured to haunt the ghostly-grey great house. In 1979, thousands of onlookers watched as a group of Jamaican and US psychics attempted to make contact with Annie Palmer. Bambos, a well-known local clairvoyant, claimed to have made contact with Annie's spirit, which guided him to a large termite's nest containing a brass urn and a voodoo doll representing the charred remains of Annie Palmer.

walk from the park is the Blue Hole, a beautiful swimming spot that is said to be bottomless. The water is a glowing turquoise blue and the pool is overhung with brightly coloured tropical blooms. There's a cheerful café on site with excellent local fare, and you can stay too in a thatched cabin or tent.

Roaring River Park. At Shrewsbury Estate, 3km (2 miles) northeast of Petersfield. Tel: (876) 957 3723. Open: Mon–Fri 9am–5pm. Admission charge. Blue Hole Garden. Tel: (876) 370 7829; www.jamaicaescapes.com. Open: daily 8am–6pm. Admission charge.

Rocklands Bird Feeding Station

Birds can be relied upon to show up each afternoon at Rocklands, situated at almost 300m (1,000ft), with a marvellous view over Montego Bay. The 'feeding station' has been here for over 30 years – the staff's knowledge of birdlife is legendary.

You can feed grassquits and saffron finches from your hands, and streamer-tailed humming birds will perch on your fingers to drink sugar-water from tiny bottles.

Rocklands, Anchovy, St James. Tel: (876) 952 2009. Open: daily 2–5pm. Admission charge.

Ron's Arawak Cave

Close to the friendly seaside community of Cousin's Cove near Negril is a large cave hung with impressive stalactite and stalagmite formations. Its endearing owner takes

visitors round the cave himself, plays the stalactites like a musical instrument and has a host of possibly true tall stories with which to entertain you. *Tel: (876) 426 6315. Open: daily 9am–5pm. Admission charge.*

Rose Hall

The most famous house in Jamaica, this grand 18th-century plantation house is perched atop a sweeping hillock carpeted in lime-green lawns. The hall's commanding presence is heightened by its thick granite walls. Inside is as cool as a well, and standing at the base of the sweeping staircase it is easy to imagine guests whirling around the high-ceilinged ballroom to a merry waltz while outside the slaves toiled beneath the evening sun.

The Georgian structure was built between 1770 and 1780 at the heyday of sugar. It fell into disuse at an early stage and was found in 1830 to be 'unoccupied save by rats, bats and owls'. It remained an imposing ruin until 1966, when a wealthy American – John Rollins, former lieutenant-governor of Delaware – restored the house to haughty grandeur.

The ballroom retains the silk wall fabric – an exact reproduction of an original designed for Marie Antoinette. The house is fully furnished with original antiques, including Hepplewhite, Sheraton and Chippendale furniture. Downstairs the dungeon has been turned into a pub straight out of *Treasure Island*.

The splendour of the Georgian house has long been overshadowed, however, by the legend of Annie Palmer, the White Witch of Rose Hall (*see pp108–9*). In her bedroom is a plantation-made, Regency-style Jamaican mahogany bed in which she was supposedly entertained by her slave lovers.
Rose Hall, PO Box 186, Montego Bay. 5km (3 miles) east of Montego Bay. Tel: (876) 953 2323. Open: daily 9am–6pm. Tours every 15 minutes.

Royal Palm Reserve

Under the jurisdiction of the Negril Area Environmental Protection Trust, this beautiful oasis has been set aside to protect the endemic Morass Royal Palm. From a wooden boardwalk you can see much of Jamaica's wildlife, including birds, butterflies, waterfowl and the endangered West Indian Whistling Duck.
Springfield Rd, Sheffield. A shuttle service operates from Negril. Tel: (876) 364 7407; www.royalpalmreserve.com. Open: daily 9am–6pm. Admission charge.

Savanna-La-Mar

Known locally as 'Sav', this is a dilapidated port town and capital of Westmoreland Parish. It was founded about 1703 at an unenviable location hemmed in by mangrove swamps, and has been destroyed several times by hurricanes.

In 1988, Hurricane Gilbert destroyed Sav's dock, along with hundreds of old, poorly constructed wooden houses (most of which were replaced by new, poorly constructed wooden houses).

Intricate cast-iron fountain at Savanna-la-Mar (the name means 'plain by the sea')

Hurricane Ivan in 2004 added further damage to Sav's waterfront, though a few of the venerable timber houses with high-pitched shingled roofs remain.

Great George Street, the broad main street, stretches inland for well over a kilometre. It terminates at the seaward end by the old fort, now swamped by sea water. More intriguing is the domed cast-iron fountain dating from 1887 opposite the courthouse.
29km (18 miles) east of Negril.

Seaford Town

A curious anomaly, Seaford Town is home to a dwindling community of fair-skinned, blue-eyed farmers of German descent.

When slavery ended, the Jamaican government encouraged European peasants to settle. Between 1834 and 1837, more than 1,000 immigrants came from North Germany; about 250 settled on Montpelier Mountain, site of today's Seaford (named after Lord Seaford, who donated the land). A newspaper of the time described Seaford as 'a perfect sink-hole'; the

The Tryall Mill waterwheel dwarfs its attendant mechanic

domestic arrangements, complained the paper, were altogether un-English!

For 150 years, the German stock has refused to integrate with black Jamaicans. They have retained their features by persistent in-breeding. Today, only about 200 whites remain (many have emigrated to Canada in recent years), the German language has gone, and only a few scraps of German folklore endure.

Tiny houses of German provenance rise up the hillsides, from which the farmers eke out a none-too-profitable existence. The cottages are reminiscent of those in Germany's Weser valley, with a distinctive gable with two small windows above the doorway. Note the house just above the Catholic Church of the Sacred Heart, with false, painted doors and windows and plants.

The church was established in 1873 by Father Tauer, who converted most residents to Catholicism.

Seaford Town Historical Mini-Museum, in the church grounds, was founded in the 1970s by Father Francis Friesen, and has maps, photographs and artefacts tracing the Germanic heritage.
36.5km (24 miles) south of Montego Bay. Tel: (876) 995 2067. Museum open by request. Admission charge.

Soldier Stone

This roadside marker at Struie was erected in honour of Private Obediah Bell Chambers by his fellow soldiers. According to the barely legible inscription, Chambers was 'cruelly butchered' when ambushed by rebellious slaves in January 1832. Local lore says that when Chambers's head was chopped off it fled and was found in Cuba.

The place is supposedly haunted. Listen for the clang of clashing swords at night!

8km (5 miles) west of Seaford Town, 34km (21 miles) south of Montego Bay.

The enchanting YS Waterfalls

Tryall Estate

This former sugar plantation, 19.5km (12 miles) west of Montego Bay, is now a grand Jamaican resort with a long beachfront and a spectacular championship golf course (site of the Johnnie Walker Pro-Am Tournament).

The sugar estate was destroyed during the slave uprising of 1831–2, but the structures were rebuilt in 1834. The mill's old waterwheel still turns under the weight of water running down a 3km- (2-mile-) long aqueduct from the Flint River.

The estate Great House is now the nucleus of the lobby and lounge of Tryall Golf, Tennis and Beach Club (*tel: (876) 956 5660; www.tryallclub.com*). A gravestone embedded in the lawn in front of the entrance is that of the head driver of the estate who was 'shot by the rebels while defending his master's property on the 8th of January 1832'. Note the cannons guarding the beach club.

YS Waterfalls

These triple-tiered cascades form a remote beauty spot reached by a jitney ride along a 3km (2-mile) track. Each fall shelters a limestone cave and tumbles into a pool good for swimming. Mosses and ferns thrive in the mists. The YS cascades lie on a 809-hectare (2,000-acre) working farm specialising in breeding tropical livestock. The land has belonged to the Browne family, descendants of the Marquis of Sligo, since 1887 (Sligo was governor of Jamaica in 1833, shortly before slavery was abolished). Near the bridge over the river you can explore the remains of the old sugar mill.

YS is a popular tour-group locale with a gift store and a thatched restaurant serving grilled dishes. Go early, before the tour buses arrive.

The curious name derives from a Gaelic word '*Wyess*', meaning 'winding', describing the course of the river. *Wyess* was abbreviated to YS and adopted as the estate mark on barrels of sugar.

1.5km (1 mile) north of Middle Quarters, 56km (35 miles) west of Mandeville. Tel: (876) 634 2454; www.ysfalls.com. Open: Tue–Sun 9.30am–3.30pm.

Walk: Montego Bay

While Mo'Bay is renowned for its beaches, it also has plenty of historical edifices to enjoy. This walk through the heart of Jamaica's premier resort town leads past the most interesting and best-preserved buildings. It ends at Mo'Bay's famous crafts market.

Allow 2 hours.

Begin at the old fort on Gloucester Ave.

1 Montego Bay Fort

This tiny fort still mounts a battery of George III cannons, green with patina. *From the fort's upper reaches, stroll to the roundabout. Follow Fort St as it swings south toward the town centre.*

2 Sam Sharpe Square

This lively square centres on a traffic island with a fountain. It also holds the

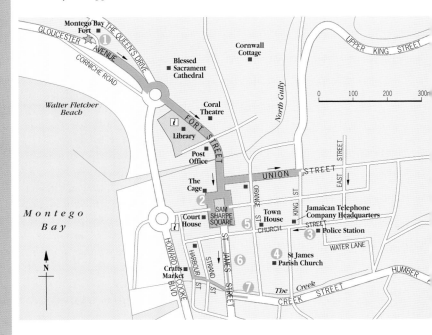

Cage, where runaway slaves and miscreants were imprisoned, and fine bronze statues of national heroes Paul Bogle and Sam Sharpe. The south side has the city's newly rebuilt civic centre and town hall.

Retrace your steps to Union St. Continue up Union St to East St. The 'Slave Ring' that once stood on the northeastern corner was most likely used for cockfighting. Turn right. Turn right again at Church St.

3 Church Street

On the corner of Church Street and Water Lane is the police station, an octagonal, two-storey plantation-style building that has wide verandas supported by square, fluted columns. Opposite, on the corner of King Street, note the gleaming white Georgian structure with a doorway lit by beautiful brass lamps.

On the junction's south side is another Georgian building – the towering, pink stucco headquarters of the Jamaican Telephone Company – with a soaring hardwood door.
Continue down Church St.

4 St James Parish Church

The tall, handsome church of white limestone is in the shape of a Greek cross. It was restored after being wrecked by an earthquake in 1957. The churchyard contains interesting graves, many in a sorry state of delapidation.

A shopkeeper hangs out her wares in a Montego Bay crafts market

5 Town House

This stately red-brick mansion at 16 Church Street dates back to 1765 and now accommodates the popular Town House Restaurant (*tel: (876) 952 2660*). *Proceed down Church St to St James St.*

6 St James Street

Mo'Bay's main shopping strip is a lively thoroughfare with sidewalk vendors and push-cart salesmen fighting to be heard above each other and the constant blaring reggae.
Proceed down St James St and take a left turn at Creek St.

7 The Dome

This unusual circular structure was built in 1837 to collect water from the stream running along Creek Street which was, until 1894, Montego Bay's only source of fresh water. It is rather dilapidated now.
Head back down Creek St towards Harbour St to the crafts market. End your walk here.

Drive: Montego Bay

A short jaunt into the rolling and rugged green hills leads to relatively isolated communities that retain remnants of their distinct culture. A working plantation and a bird sanctuary also lie tucked in the hills. The occasional sweeping vistas beg extra film!

Allow 4 hours, including stops.

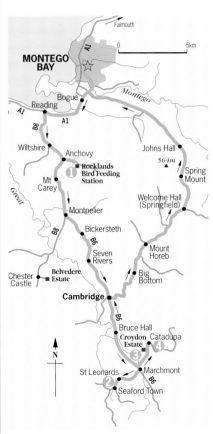

Depart Mo'Bay via Barnett St (A1) westward to Reading. Turn left and follow the B8 uphill to Anchovy via a narrow limestone gorge. After 3km (2 miles), turn left for Rocklands Bird Feeding Station (the short climb is steep and potholed).

1 Rocklands Bird Feeding Station

A wide variety of birds, including the doctor bird, Jamaica's national bird, can be relied upon to show up mid-afternoons for feeding time. With luck you can have a humming bird feed from your hand. (*See also pp84–5.*) *Return to the B8. Turn left and continue south 5km (3 miles) to Montpelier. Turn left on to the B6 opposite the Texaco station (follow the sign to Croydon Estate). Beyond Cambridge are dramatic vistas of serrated mountains and deep-forested valleys. Sixteen kilometres (10 miles) beyond Montpelier turn right at the 4-way junction at Marchmont. Three kilometres (2 miles) further on a sign reads: 'Now Entering Seaford.*

A German Town Founded in 1835.'
Continue to the T-junction and then
turn right for Seaford Town.

2 Seaford Town

This neat hillside settlement has gabled
wooden houses reminiscent of cottages
in Germany's Weser valley. One-third of
Seaford's inhabitants are of German
stock: blond haired, blue eyed, but their
numbers are dwindling. The Historical
Museum next to the Sacred Heart
Catholic Church illustrates the town's
heritage (drive to the Sacred Mission,
for the key). (*See also p112.*)
Return to Marchmont. Cross the junction
and follow the road to the right towards
Catadupa. Turn left at the sign for
Croydon Estate.

3 Croydon Estate

Croydon grows coffee, citrus and
pineapples on 53 hectares (132 acres) of
terraces. A 'see, hear, touch and taste'
tour includes a Jamaican lunch served
atop a hill with a commanding view of
the valley (*tel: (876) 979 8267;*
www.croydonplantation.com). Return to
the road to Catadupa; turn left into
town. The road beyond Catadupa is
suitable only for jeeps; as one local says,
'Road bad to Hell, mon!'

4 Catadupa

This erstwhile coffee-growing centre
has gone into decline since the railway
shut down in 1992. The station still
stands, as does the factory for washing
and pulping coffee beans, and the town
makes for an interesting visit.
Return to Marchmont and Cambridge.
Turn right for Mount Horeb and
Welcome Hall (locally called Springfield;
the road is not signposted). The well-
paved, lonesome road switchbacks
through dramatic karst country of deep
troughs and conical hillocks. Turn right
10km (6 miles) beyond Cambridge; then
left, 5km (3 miles) further, at Welcome
Hall. Continue downhill to Montego Bay.

Drive: Montego Bay

Known as Mo'Bay, lively Montego Bay is the best known of Jamaica's resorts

South central

The south coast is a secret corner that stands on the verge of discovery. Unblemished as yet are its secluded beaches, hidden coves, soaring cliffs, charming fishing villages and, above all, its serene mountain scenery. The region offers a contrast to the traditional sun-and-sand vacation. Mandeville was the first town in Jamaica to promote community-based tourism, and the region is now known for its low-key atmosphere and lack of brash resorts. There isn't, yet, a single all-inclusive hotel in the south, though the Sandals chain has edged very close with an enormous property near Whitehouse.

South central Jamaica

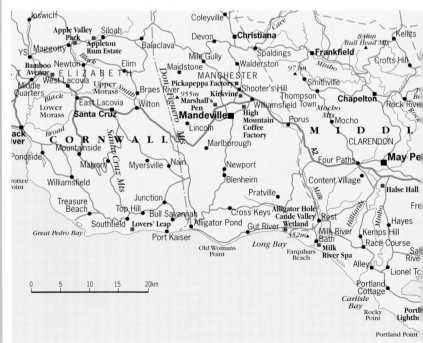

The south coast is basically a great basin rimmed by mountains. The flat fertile plain and verdant highland valleys constitute the 'breadbasket of Jamaica'. The geographic contrasts, however, are startling. To the west the waters of the Black River gather in great swamps, known as the Great Morass. Guided tours take you into a realm known for its rich birdlife and crocodiles. Here, too, shading the A2, is Bamboo Avenue, a 3km (2-mile) glade of giant bamboos.

Following the A2 east, you snake until eventually you arrive on a plateau hidden away in the Don Figuerero Mountains. At its centre sits Mandeville, which retains a dash of old England. Further south lies sleepy Malvern, a refreshingly cool hilltop treasure.

Here, 600m (2,000ft) up in the mountains where the air is redolent with night-blooming jasmine, the roads that cut through the Mocho, Don Figuerero and Santa Cruz Mountains rise, dip and curve through very untropical terrain.

Tourists may also be surprised to find themselves surrounded by cacti, and parched semi-savanna. There is water here. To sample it, visit Milk River Spa, where the mineral springs are more potent than any in Europe. The waters must be healthy, for rare manatees and crocodiles survive amid the coastal estuaries.

Further east lies Spanish Town, fascinating for history buffs. The Spanish, the English and the Africans all left their mark on Jamaica's erstwhile capital city. Sadly, Hurricane Gilbert dealt the town a devastating blow in 1988. The Cathedral Church of St James, however, has lost none of its stunning if simple glory.

Fishing is a staple of the south coast. Beaches are highlighted by Treasure Beach, anchored by one of the quaintest and quietest fishing villages of all. Nearby are the awesome cliffs of Lovers' Leap.

The stock of hotel rooms is small, with none of the high-rises of the major resort centres. Choose a cosy inn by a lonesome beach – you can walk for ages without seeing another soul!

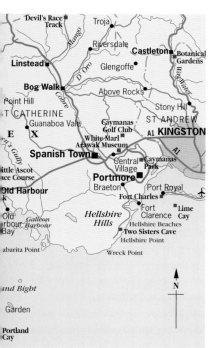

Mandeville

Mandeville, capital of Manchester Parish, is named after Lord Mandeville, whose father, the Duke of Manchester, was governor of Jamaica in the early 1800s. The town is perched at a crisp 610m (2,000ft) elevation. Established in 1816, it served for much of the century as a hill station for British regiments.

Mandeville has long been favoured by expatriates for its year-round salubrious spring-like climate. A century ago, anyone who was anyone holidayed here. Later it became a retirement haven for English folk who found that it reminded them of home. The discovery of bauxite in the 1950s fostered the influx of a new breed of expatriate – North Americans.

Today, Mandeville (population 35,000) is the fifth-largest town in Jamaica. It is an important agricultural centre and dormitory town for two aluminium companies that have laid out expansive residential areas.

Lying 98km (61 miles) west of Kingston, the town is surrounded by hills reminiscent of England, and vales laid out for citrus production (particularly the ortanique, a locally developed hybrid, part orange, part tangerine).

Bloomfield Great House

This popular restaurant offers a bird's-eye view of Mandeville. The restaurant, housed in an old restored mansion, has a well-chosen display of Jamaican art on its walls.
Bloomfield Gardens. Tel: (876) 962 7130.

Cecil Charlton Park

Mandeville's lively town square, locally called The Green, was recently renamed Cecil Charlton Park after the former mayor (*see below*). Dominating the square is the Parish Church of St Mark, built of limestone, and, opposite, the Georgian court-house, with an attractive horseshoe staircase and a portico on Doric columns. Both date from 1820. The old rectory, next to the courthouse, is Mandeville's oldest structure. To the east **Mandeville Hotel**, a former army officer's quarters from 1875, claims to be the oldest hotel in Jamaica.

Huntingdon Summit

The strange, pagoda-like mansion crowning Huntingdon Summit, 5km (3 miles) south of the town, is the ostentatious home of Cecil C Charlton, millionaire politician, farmer and Mayor of Mandeville for over 20 years until 1986.

A highlight is an indoor pond connected to an outdoor swimming pool by an underground tunnel. *Ring ahead for an appointment. Tel: (876) 962 7758. Open: daily, except Wed & Sat. Free admission, but a donation to a local charity is welcome.*

Mrs Stephenson's Garden

The headquarters of the venerated Manchester Horticultural Society is a private garden filled with anthuriums and orchids. Carmen Stephenson will show you round herself if you call first to make an appointment.
25 New Green Rd. Tel: (876) 962 2909.

Williamsfield

This hamlet that nestles in a vale at the base of Shooter's Hill, 8km (5 miles) northeast of Mandeville, is the home of the High Mountain Coffee Factory. *Tel: (876) 962 4211. Tours by prior arrangement.*

Kirkvine Works

Kirkvine Works, northeast of Mandeville, was opened in 1952 as Jamaica's first aluminium plant – it remains the island's largest. The owner, WINDALCO (West Indies Alumina Company), welcomes visitors with one day's notice (*tel: (876) 961 7024*). Their massive landholdings – 12,500 hectares (31,000 acres) under rehabilitation or not yet mined – are given over to livestock and citrus.

The courthouse at Mandeville was built by slaves from limestone blocks

A fisherman shows off some of his catch at Alligator Pond

Pickapeppa Factory

The Pickapeppa Factory makes the famous sinus-searing gourmet sauce, conjured from a closely guarded recipe using tropical fruits and spices.
At the junction of the B4, B5 and B6, 10km (6 miles) northeast of Mandeville. Tel: (876) 603 3441; www.pickapeppa.com. Admission charge. Tours by appointment.

SWA Craft Centre

Unemployed local girls are trained here to make crafts – on sale in the centre – and to cook tasty cakes and tarts. If you visit you'll get a chance to chat to the friendly girls and find out about their daily lives.
7 North Racecourse, behind the Manchester Shopping Centre.

Alligator Pond

Dugout canoes still line the beach at this fishing village, 16km (10 miles) south of Mandeville. The early-morning fish market adds additional colour. Hungry? Take your pick of stalls selling bammy, fresh fish and lobster. A local fisherman will be happy to take you out fishing for a fee.

Long Bay, to the east, is lined by mangrove swamps, a habitat of manatees, or sea cows, the gentle and sluggish marine mammals that gave rise to the legend of mermaids during Columbus's time. Numerous during Taino times, the harmless creatures, which grow to 4.3m (14ft) long, have since been decimated for their hide, meat and blubber.

Alligator Hole is a wildlife preserve popular with waterfowl. At Gut River, a freshwater river emerges from a small cave. The refreshingly cool water is reportedly good for swimming. The nibble you feel is only a toothy, though shy and retiring crocodile (locally called alligators).

Bamboo Avenue

This glade of frilly bamboos towers over the road. The 3km- (2-mile-) long sun-dappled nave is over a century old, despite frequent batterings by storms. The grove, a well-known landmark between Middle Quarters and Lacovia, is maintained by staff from the Hope Botanical Gardens. It is extremely photogenic and well worth the drive.

Christiana

This small market town is surrounded by lush agricultural land cultivated by light-skinned farmers of German provenance, the offspring of mercenaries who received land grants in Jamaica after fighting for Britain during the American War of Independence. The main crop is potatoes.

Note the imposing police station and courthouse, dating from 1896, as well as the intriguing Moravian church, built about 1891.
16km (10 miles) north of Mandeville.

Colbeck Castle

The ruined 'castle', 3km (2 miles) northwest of Old Harbour, was built in the late 18th century and named after – though not built by – Colonel John Colbeck, an early English settler. The grey-brick mansion is now but a shell surrounded by tobacco fields. Note the underground slave quarters at each corner.

Great Morass (Upper and Lower)

This vast area, a watery swamp fed by the Black River and its many tributaries, suits its name – The Morass forms a rare remnant habitat for fish, especially tarpon and snook, and birds such as egrets, jacanas and even ospreys. It is also Jamaica's major refuge of 'alligators' (American crocodiles) that sun themselves on the muddy riverbanks.

Various schemes to drain and develop the swamps date back to 1783, when the British attempted to settle some loyalist refugees from Carolina, but local opposition to the scheme led to its failure. Even today, the locals make great play of the fact that even a settler whose name was Frogge found the area too damp. Locals have found success in growing *ganja* (marijuana), and a company called Jamculture raises shrimp and fish.

Halse Hall

Splendidly situated amid a rolling plantation, Halse Hall is one of the

Hurricanes have repeatedly damaged Bamboo Avenue, but continuing efforts ensure that it is well maintained

oldest continuously occupied Great Houses in Jamaica. The pretty stone and wood structure was built as a fortified home by a British soldier, Thomas Halse. Beneath it lies a Spanish foundation that dates back to when the property was known by its original name of Hato de Buena Vista (Ranch of the Beautiful View). It was recently restored and is furnished with period pieces.

5km (3 miles) south of May Pen, on the road to Lionel Town. Tour by prior permission. Tel: (876) 986 2215. Admission charge.

Hellshire Beaches

This long strand of talcum-fine sand fringes a barren promontory southwest of Kingston. Quiet during the week, it's usually heaving at the weekends with sound-systems and a party atmosphere. Reggae concerts and informal soccer games are often held on the beach. As well as water-sports facilities there's a small, pleasant hotel. But the reason Kingstonians flock here is for the local speciality – fried fish and festival, a kind of savoury doughnut – said to be the best of its kind in the whole of Jamaica. On Sundays you'll have to queue for food but the wait is well worth while.

Fort Clarence Beach

While Hellshire is an institution in Jamaica, its neighbouring beach is much more low-key and is privately owned. Hence the clean changing rooms and presence of lifeguards on duty at the weekends. There are several snack shops and a bar.

Open: Mon–Fri 10am–5pm, Sat & Sun 8am–7pm. Admission charge.

Salt Pond

Salt Pond, in the lee of Fort Clarence, was once a fishing ground of Arawak Indians; abundant fish still provide food for a family of crocodiles that lives in the mangrove swamps. Swimming is not recommended!

Hellshire Hills

These limestone hills backing the Hellshire Beaches lure ramblers and nature lovers. The porous bedrock, called honeycomb, soaks up the little rain it receives; the surface soil is therefore quite thin, and hospitable only to cactus and thorny shrub.

Trails lead through the dry tropical deciduous forest and spiny scrubland which form the heart of a nature reserve. Iguanas, extinct elsewhere on the island, are commonly seen. The hills' unique wildlife includes the endangered Jamaican coney, a nocturnal mammal often called the Jamaican rabbit. To the southeast, mangrove swamps are inhabited by manatees.

Caves pock the landscape, one of which – **Two Sisters Cave** – is a tourist attraction. Rock-carved steps lead you down to a pool where river bass thrive. From the observation platform you can look across the shimmering waters to a rock carving left by Arawak Indians.

Urbanisation is fast encroaching. Portmore is the most developed of a series of dormitory communities being developed as suburbs of Kingston.

Lacovia

Lacovia, immediately east of Bamboo Avenue, is a one-street village (the longest on the island) that sprawls along the A2 and is divided into West Lacovia, East Lacovia and Lacovia Tombstone. The English and Spanish battled for the ford over the Black River in 1655.

In 1723, Lacovia was named the capital of St Elizabeth but lost its title after a long dispute with Black River – the courts and other functions alternated between the two towns for half a century. Several tombstones attest that Lacovia was at that time mostly inhabited by Jews. It grew to be an important river port from which log-wood and fustic (both used to extract dyes) were shipped. On the road in front of the Texaco station are tombstones of two soldiers who killed each other in a duel in 1738.

Lovers' Leap

Not for the faint-hearted! Here, the Santa Cruz Mountains shoulder right up to the coast and a 52m (170ft) cliff plunges sheer to the ocean. Far below, waves crash ashore on the jagged rocks.

Climb the steps to the right of the restaurant for spectacular views along the coast. From on high, the blue Caribbean stretches as far as the eye can see. You can make eye-to-eye contact with buzzards – John Crows – that soar on the thermals.

According to legend, the spot is named after two lovers – slaves – who

Lovers' Leap – a view to a death if the legend is to be believed

The pleasant environs of Deep Dene School

had been forbidden to meet by their respective owners. The illicit lovers met anyway and, when about to be captured here, leapt to their deaths rather than be split apart.

Adjacent is a red-and-white-hooped lighthouse. There is a good restaurant onsite with an open-air terrace that takes in the fabulous view. It's a great place to watch the sun slide into the sea at the end of the day. There's also a small gift shop and museum.
Tel: (876) 965 6577. Open: daily 8.30am–sunset. Free admission.

Malvern

Off the tourist path but well worth seeking out, Malvern straddles the Santa Cruz mountains 730m (2,400ft) above sea level, 17.5km (11 miles) south of Santa Cruz. Its crisp setting is extremely picturesque. Once a resort town popular with the well-to-do,

today Malvern is a prosperous agricultural community with several intriguing old stone buildings. Look for Deep Dene, on the road to Black River. It has a steep, sloping roof and low veranda fringed with gingerbread trim – the essence of picture-postcard pretty. Deep Dene is one of three acclaimed and historic schools, established by charitable trusts for the education of indigent children.

The mountain roads that lead to Malvern offer spectacular vistas down over the bright-green plains, and occasional peeks across the deep valley towards Mandeville.

Marshall's Pen

At the heart of this 120-hectare (300-acre) cattle farm, one of the most acclaimed cattle-rearing centres in the Caribbean, is a well-kept 18th-century Great House that once belonged to the Earl of Balcarres, Governor of Jamaica (1795–1801). The home, off Winston Jones Highway north of Mandeville, is filled with antique treasures, as well as a stamp and shell collection. Beyond the beautiful garden is a bird sanctuary and nature reserve replete with reptiles, butterflies and other insects.

Overnight stays – birders only – can be arranged through the owner, Anne Sutton. Dr Sutton is a prominent ornithologist. Her son leads birding trips along the nature trails.
Marshall's Pen, PO Box 58, Mandeville. Tel: (876) 962 7758. Open: by prior appointment only. Admission charge.

May Pen

This market town midway between Mandeville and Spanish Town lies at the heart of a highly developed agricultural district. Call in on Friday or Saturday for the lively market. The annual Denbigh Show, Jamaica's major agricultural show, is held here in the first week of August.

An American air base was established nearby at Vernham Field during World War II. Today it is used for occasional autoracing and illegal marijuana trafficking – for this reason it's not a place to drop in casually!

Milk River Bath

If Jamaica's warm seas do not relax you, head for Milk River Bath, Jamaica's foremost spa. The hot waters which emerge from the base of the Carpenter Mountains are the most radioactive waters on earth – three times more so than those of Karlovy Vary in the Czech Republic, and nine times that of Bath in England.

An immersion is supposed to cure rheumatism, eczema, sciatica, lumbago, gout and a host of other complaints. The recommended treatment is three soaks per day, each no longer than 20 minutes. A large swig of murky water is part of the cure (presumably, a good way to increase your half-life!). 'Overwhelming vitality is restored', claims the homely Milk River Bath Hotel (*tel: (876) 902 4657*).

The water's miraculous properties were discovered by a slave who had been lashed and left for dead. When he reappeared, miraculously healed, estate owner Jonathan Ludford built the first baths in 1794.

Milk River is popular at weekends with Kingstonians. Choose between the rather dingy hotel spa, where massages are also available, or a public spa and swimming pool nearby (*open: weekends & public holidays, 10am–6pm*).

The primitive road continues past tall cacti to a quaint fishing village where the river meets Farquhars Beach. The mangrove swamps here harbour American crocodiles (alligators). You can watch fishermen bringing in their catch and enjoy a simple meal in one of the rustic restaurants run by Rastas. *45km (28 miles) southeast of Mandeville.*

Old Harbour

Old Harbour, on the A2 midway between May Pen and Spanish Town, is a sleepy market town. At its heart is an elegant iron Victorian clock tower topped by a filigree crown, and it is so superbly maintained that you can set your watch by its time. Nearby is a funky fishing village.

Tubs full of green vegetables in the market

Spanish Town

Jamaica's third-largest town, 22.5km (14 miles) west of Kingston, is the cradle of the island's modern history. The Spanish established their capital here in 1523, centred on a plaza – today's Parade. When the British captured the city in 1655, Cromwell's soldiers razed the Spanish buildings, which were gradually replaced with structures of surprising elegance. The town – now run-down – remained Jamaica's capital until 1872.

The Parade is surrounded by decrepit Georgian buildings; the garden, shaded by tall palms, was ravaged by Hurricane Gilbert and has also gone to ruin.

Of note are the colourful market; King Street, with Georgian houses with jalousies and 'coolers'; a venerable though neglected military barracks dating from 1791; and an iron bridge over the Rio Cobre, shipped from England in 1801 and the oldest surviving cast-iron bridge in the Americas.

Rodney Memorial

This noble edifice on the north side of the Parade celebrates Admiral Rodney's victory over a French and Spanish invasion fleet in April 1782. A marble statue of Rodney dressed in a Roman toga is enclosed by a 'temple' with a cupola. Relief panels on the pediment depict the battle. Two brass cannons from the French flagship flank the statue (by eminent English artist John Bacon).

Behind the memorial are the Archives Office and Records Office, housing important historical and legal documents. The empty red-brick shell opposite was once the courthouse. This was built in 1819 but destroyed by fire in 1986.

Classical grandeur in Spanish Town: the white-stucco Rodney Memorial building

Old Kings House

An impressive porticoed Georgian façade is all that remains of the once-magnificent red-brick structure built in 1762 as the official residence of the governors of Jamaica. It, too, was destroyed by fire, in 1925.

Opposite, on the east side, is the former House of Assembly, built in 1760. The impressive brick building with pillared wooden balcony overhanging a shady colonnade now houses the offices of the St Catherine Parish Council.

People's Museum of Craft and Technology

The museum, operated by the Institute of Jamaica, is housed in the old stables of Old Kings House. It provides an intriguing entrée to early Jamaican culture. There are reconstructions of a smithy or farrier's, plus early carpenters' tools, Indian corn grinders and cassava press, pottery, baskets, and so on, and a model of the original Old Kings House. The grounds contain an old sugar press, coffee huskers, corn grinders and delapidated old carriages. There is also a restaurant and bar.
Tel: (876) 907 0322. Museum open: Mon–Thur 9.30am–4.30pm, Fri 9.30am–3.30pm. Admission charge.

Cathedral of St Jago de la Vega

One of the prettiest churches in Jamaica, the red-brick cathedral is topped by an octagonal steeple with Corinthian columns. The church dates from 1714. It was built on the site of a 1523 Spanish church, the first cathedral in the New World. The original black-and-white chequered floor is studded with graves dating from 1662.

The beautiful interior features wooden fluted pillars, carved pews and choir stalls, beamed ceiling, stained glass and a large organ from 1849.

Treasure Beach

If there is treasure to be found in Jamaica, it lies on the south coast at Treasure Beach, a seemingly endless crescent of coral-coloured sand. There are several places to stay, including the endearingly off-beat Jake's (*tel: (876) 965 3000; www.islandoutpost.com*).

Many of the fishing pirogues are worked by blue-eyed descendants of Scottish seamen shipwrecked in the 19th century.
30.5km (19 miles) southeast of Black River.

Taino Museum

Worth a peek, the museum houses a major collection of Taino Indian finds. It is sited on the largest Amerindian settlement in Jamaica, and includes middens, a reconstruction of a Taino village, plus comprehensive displays that tell of the social and economic life of the Taino Indians.
Off the Nelson Mandela Freeway, 3km (2 miles) east of Spanish Town. Open: Mon–Thur 8.30am–5pm; Fri 8.30am–4pm. Closed: weekends. Admission charge.

Drive: Mandeville

This country drive leads into the heart of some of Jamaica's prettiest scenery. Parts are reminiscent of England, with lime-green meadows lined by limestone walls, and sheep and cattle grazing the margins each side. Elsewhere are sugar-cane fields, flat and green as a billiard table, backed by the forest-clad conical hills of the Cockpit Country, traditionally one of the most inaccessible and remote areas of the island. Even today roads are few and little-used.

Allow 4–5 hours, including stops.

From Mandeville, the centre of a rural and recently industrialised area and built in the style of an English country town, follow New Green Rd north to Mark Post. Turn left on to the B6 1.5km (1 mile) beyond Martin's Hill Orchid Sanctuary. Continue for 6.5km (4 miles) and turn left at the sign for Comfort

Hall. Follow the sign for Balaclava, then turn right at kilometre 21 (mile 13) and again about 6.5km (4 miles) further on. The road winds through a broad valley and Siloah, a charming village of old wooden houses. Beyond Siloah, the Appleton Rum Estate factory is on your right.

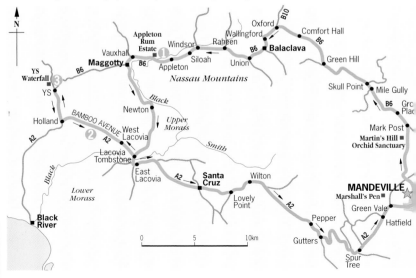

1 Appleton Rum Estate

The Appleton estate has been growing sugar cane and turning it into rum since 1749. The Appleton Estate Rum Tour provides an inside look at the distillery and the distilling process. Newly cut cane can be seen being transported by JCBs then rolled through giant crushers to release the juice. After being boiled at very high temperatures, the juice is crystallised into sugar using massive centrifuges. While here, visitors can taste the fresh-pressed cane juice and molasses, as well as savour the famous rums. There is a restaurant and bar on the site (*tel: (876) 963 9215; www.appletonrum.com*).
Continue west for 0.8km (½ mile) to a roundabout. Here turn left for Maggotty, then follow the road south to Lacovia Tombstone, where a tombstone beside the petrol station commemorates an English soldier, Thomas Jordan Spencer, an ancestor of both Winston Churchill and Princess Diana. Turn right on to the A2 and follow the road west for 3km (2 miles) to reach Bamboo Ave.

2 Bamboo Avenue

An extremely photogenic, 3km- (2-mile-) long glade of bushy bamboos that curve over to form a cool, green tunnel. The giant bamboos date back to the 19th century. Fields of citrus fruit and sugar cane flank the road. (*See also p122.*)
About 1.5km (1 mile) west of Bamboo Ave turn right at Holland on to a dirt road leading to YS Waterfall. The ruler-straight track leads past a papaya plantation and meadows grazed by Red Poll cattle.

3 YS Waterfall

YS Falls in St Elizabeth Parish is one of Jamaica's largest, most scenic and least-known cataracts. The beautiful cascade descends 37m (120ft) like a staircase, with cool pools for swimming. The falls are on the YS Estate, which breeds racehorses and raises cattle. It also has a gift store and an excellent restaurant. (*See also p113.*)
Retrace your route back to the A2, which will take you back to Mandeville.

The Appleton estate rum distillery is both the oldest and the biggest in Jamaica

Pirates

Pirates fill the most colourful chapter in Jamaica's chromatic history. For almost a century these wild and ruthless sea rovers raped, pillaged and plundered their way around the Caribbean.

They began life in the mid-1600s as 'buccaneers' (after the *boucan*, a wooden rack used to dry hides and meat), a band of sedentary misfits who congregated on Tortuga, off Hispaniola.

When the Spaniards drove them out they washed ashore in Jamaica, formed the Confederacy of the Brethren of the Coast, and turned to ruthless plunder. Success soon swelled their numbers and fostered the rise of Port Royal as their base.

Nourished by booty, Port Royal rapidly evolved (or degenerated) into a hive of debauchery known as the 'wickedest city in the world'. John Esquemeling, himself a buccaneer, wrote that he saw one fellow 'give unto a common strumpet five hundred pieces-of-eight only that he might see her naked'.

When the Second Dutch War began in 1665, the English legalised the buccaneers as 'privateers' to harass Spanish and Dutch shipping.

The pirates reached their zenith under Henry Morgan, a rapacious Welsh sea captain who led a ruinous rape of the Spanish Main, crowned by the sacking and destruction of Panama in 1671.

Eventually Morgan was knighted, named Jamaica's lieutenant-governor, and charged with suppressing the buccaneers.

He held this post for six years until he fell out of favour. He then lived in uproarious drunkenness for another seven years and possibly died from liver failure, but it was very unusual for a pirate to reach retirement age.

Though Port Royal was destroyed by an earthquake in 1692, pirates multiplied. Their voracity and sadism increased in proportion. No vessel, town or plantation was safe.

This era of infamy bred such colourful figures as Blackbeard (Edwin Teach), who carried lighted fuses in his beard, and Calico Jack (Jack Rackham), so-called because of his penchant for calico underwear. In 1718, Blackbeard was captured and his head hung from the mainmast of his ship; Rackham was captured and executed in 1720 and his body left to rot in an iron cage near Port Royal.

Henry Morgan

Captain Henry Morgan was of all, the most celebrated Buccaneer. His association with Port Royal was key to its growth in trade and later, as a naval station. Morgan made several rams on the Spanish Main, the most spectacular being on Panama City, which in the 1670s was brimming with the gold, silver and gems of the Inca Empire and splendid Spanish Cathedrals. His attack was said to have been the most destructive and bloody pillage in buccaneering history. Treasures estimated at 750,000 pieces of eight, including slaves and ransomed hostages were said to have arrived at Port Royal from it. For this Morgan was named Lieutenant Governor of Jamaica by the King of England.

Many tales of pirates and plunder are based on real-life characters of Jamaican history such as the notorious Henry Morgan

Getting away from it all

*'Never had I seen a land so beautiful.
Now I knew where the writers of the Bible
had got their description of Paradise.
They had come here to Jamaica.'*

ERROL FLYNN

My Wicked, Wicked Ways, 1959

Appleton Rum Estate tour

Taste-full describes this half-day excursion by tour bus. After skirting the wild Cockpit Country, you arrive at the Appleton Rum Estate and distillery, set alongside the Black River in a lovely green valley surrounded by cane fields and mountains. Here, a tour reveals the secrets behind Jamaica's most potent elixir.

Inside the distillery visitors get to sample freshly pressed cane juice as well as molasses, 'wet sugar', 'high wine' – the intermediate stages of the rum-making process – and finally flavourful rum, which has been blended here since 1749.

The tour includes hotel transfers in Montego Bay, plus a picnic lunch and complimentary rum punch in an air-conditioned lounge (*see p98*). *Jamaica Estate Tours Ltd, c/o Appleton Estate, Siloah, St Elizabeth. Tel: (876) 963 9215; www.appletonrum.com. Admission charge.*

Blue Mountain Downhill Bicycle Tour

For information contact: *Blue Mountain Tours Ltd, 121 Main St, Ocho Rios. Tel: (876) 974 7075; www.bmtoursja.com*

The Forres Park Hotel in Mavis Bank also arranges cycling tours of the Blue Mountains (*www.forrespark.com*). *For further information on cycling in Jamaica, contact the Jamaican Cycling Federation (www.jamaicacycling.com).*

Coffee factory tours

Call in at a coffee plantation for a pick-me-up. Jamaica's exalted Blue Mountain coffee (*see pp44–5*) is grown, processed and milled at the **Mavis Bank (Central) Coffee Factory** in Mavis Bank. A tour concludes in the tasting room where a professional taster will teach you the etiquette of appreciation. After sampling the aromatic roasts you are sure to pull out your wallet. Coffee direct from the factory sells for about one-fifth the price in the UK or the USA (tours by appointment; *tel: (876) 977 8005)*.

Also in the Blue Mountains is the Old Tavern Coffee Estate which produces some of the best coffee in the area. Tours of the picturesque estate can be arrranged in advance. *Tel: (876) 929 1775; www.oldtaverncoffee.com*

In the central highlands follow your nose to the **High Mountain Coffee Factory** (*tel: (876) 963 4211)* at Williamsfield, near Mandeville. The factory specialises in High Mountain coffee, which is a lighter, sweeter brew than Blue Mountain (tours by appointment only).

Getting away from it all

Packing the aromatic Blue Mountain coffee

Community tourism

Seeking an alternative to a 'sun and sand' holiday? **Countrystyle International** (*tel: (876) 962 7758/488 7207; www. countrystylecommunity tourism.com*), which is based at the Astra Inn in Mandeville, offers holiday experiences aimed at sponsoring development among communities traditionally bypassed by the tourist market. Visits with local families and accommodation in rural homes introduce you to Jamaican community life and culture.

Cuba

Europeans and Canadians have fallen in love with Cuba's silky sands, satin waters and trove of colonial treasures. Several Jamaican companies offer tours to Havana, Santiago or Varadero, a 20km- (12-mile-) long finger of land with powder-white beaches that outdo even Negril's. Cigar factories, louche cabarets, old *yanqui* cars – Cuba has a variety of attractions.

Caribic Vacations (*tel: (876) 953 9895; www.caribicvacations.com*) offers package tours to Havana, the Cuban capital and the 'Paris of the Caribbean'. Its narrow, cobblestoned streets brim with baroque and neoclassical cathedrals, palaces, museums and wide, palm-lined boulevards.

Cuba Jump (*tel: (876) 971 3859; www.marzonca.com*) specialises in well-priced hotel packages to the main resort areas of Cuba.

Tropical Tours (*tel: (876) 953 9100; www.tropicaltours-ja.com*) have a range of tours to Havana, the historic city of Trinidad – one of Cuba's most atmospheric places – and the beach resort of Varadero.

Your passport is required – it will not be stamped by the Cuban authorities.

Environmental tours

Ecotourism – travel that contributes to the conservation of natural environments – is growing in popularity in Jamaica.

The two-hour **Black River Safari** explores the Upper and Lower Morass, the biggest and most diverse swamp system in the Caribbean. Ten- and 25-seater motor launches leave the town of Black River for a 11km (7-mile) guided tour through a region that resembles the Florida Everglades. Over 100 species of birds roost here, including herons, ospreys, chocolate-hued jacanas and snow-white egrets. With luck you may see freshwater turtles and crocodiles eyeing you leerily, as well as shrimp fishermen plying their trade in dugout canoes hung with shrimp pots. Colourful water lilies and delicate hyacinths grow in abundance. Several companies run tours up the river the most interesting, with genuine scientific content, is run by wetland ecologist Lloyd Linton. *Contact IRIE Safaris (tel: (876) 965 2221).*

Chukka Caribbean Adventures is a hugely successful and well-organised

'adventure tour' company with a strong environmental conscience and was awarded Green Globe certified status in 2006. The company has two Jamaican bases – in Hanover and St Mary – and offers a wide range of outdoor activities including biking, horse-riding along the beach, river tubing and kayaking.
Tel: (876) 953 6699;
www.chukkacaribbean.com
Sun Venture Tours is an eco-friendly tour company based in Kingston which specialises in trips for nature lovers. Birdwatching, hiking and caving are part of a long list of activities and imaginative tours.
Tel: (876) 960 6685;
www.sunventuretours.com

Unique Jamaica is an ecotourism umbrella operation that brings together a range of tours and holiday packages specialising in exploring the natural beauty of Jamaica. Tours include trips to an organic farm, the Greencastle Estate in St Mary, and to the Elysium Forest Sanctuary in Lethe.
Tel: (876) 929 7895;
www.uniquejamaica.com

Helicopter tours

If you're feeling flush, **Island Hoppers** (*tel: (876) 974 1285*) is a helicopter charter company, based in Ocho Rios, which will whizz you over the island for a hefty fee. Standard tours include the one-hour 'Jamaican Showcase' which flies over Port Royal, Kingston, the Blue

Bamboo rafts are an ingenious way to traverse the calm waters

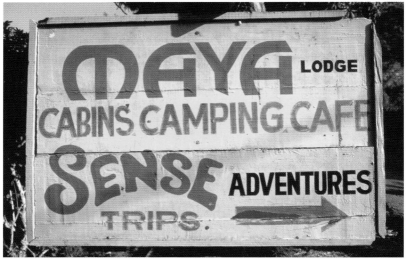

For the Blue Mountains, start from the Maya Lodge and Hiking Centre in Kingston

Mountains and Port Maria. Obviously, the views are outstanding! Helicopters can also be chartered by the hour so you can create your own aerial tour of Jamaica.

Hiking

Jamaica is laced with thousands of miles of trails that serve both locals and adventurous Indiana Joneses.

The best hiking is in the **Blue and John Crow Mountains National Park**, where trails are categorised as guided, non-guided or wilderness. Streams and waterfalls are abundant, as is wildlife rarely seen elsewhere in the island. Many trails are maintained by the **Forestry Department**.

The park is run by the Jamaican Conservation and Development Trust (29 Dumbarton Ave, Kingston 10. Tel: (876) *960 2848; www.jcdt.org.jm) and there are local ranger stations in Hollywell Recreational Park and Portland Gap in the Blue Mountains, and in Millbank in the Rio Grande Valley.*

All of the small hotels in the Blue Mountains offer a series of hikes in the area and can procure good local guides. These include Forres Park (*www.forrespark.com*) and Lime Tree Farm (*www.limetreefarm.com*) in Mavis Bank, which is a good starting point for many of the trails. The Natural History Society of Jamaica, based at the Mona campus of the University of the West Indies (*tel: (876) 977 6938*), sometimes organises treks into the park.

Also, look out for the books *A Hiker's Guide to the Blue Mountains* by Bill Wilcox and *The Blue Mountain*

Guide by Dr Margaret Hodges. (*See Blue Mountains Hike, p40.*)

The Grand Ridge of the Blue Mountains Trail links trails from the official starting point at Morces Gap, in the west, with the John Crow Mountains. Vinegar Hill Trail crosses the Blue Mountains north to south from Chepstowe, near Buff Bay, ending in Kingston. The route takes in Cinchona, Catherine's Peak and Hollywell. Another rugged trail leads from Bath Fountain across the John Crows to Millbank, 32km (20 miles) south of Port Antonio. You can even make the arduous hike to Nanny Town, after paying a courtesy call on the Maroon Colonel in Moore Town – he can arrange a guide.

Several tour companies, based in Port Antonio, organise hikes into the Rio Grande Valley and on to the John Crow Mountains. The best are **Grand Valley Tours** (*tel: (876) 993 4116; www.portantoniojamaica.com*) and **Valley Hikes** (*tel: (876) 993 3881*).

The **Fairy Glades** and **Fern Walk** trails above Newcastle invite hikers to discover the fascinating flora and fauna unique to montane cloud forest.

The Malvern Hills near Mandeville are another popular hiking spot. Trails also lace the Hellshire Hills. Much of the Cockpit Country remains unexplored and trailless; it is not wise to hike alone here. You can hire a guide in Windsor, from where a trail leads to Troy.

Many campers and hikers head for the Blue Mountains

Getting away from it all

Another trail begins at Sign Great House, east of Montego Bay, and follows the Montego River. It is always wise to hire a guide.

The **Jamaica Survey Department** (*231½ Charles St, Kingston; tel: (876) 922 6630; www.nla.gov.jm*) publishes 1:50,000 topographical maps.

Hilton High Day tour

The 'Up, Up and Buffet' tour is still fun, though it no longer includes a brief ride in a tethered hot-air balloon. Your venue is a 145-hectare (360-acre)

former banana plantation, Hilton, in St Leonards, reached via a scenic drive from Montego Bay. The hilltop location overlooks the German settlement at Seaford, visited as part of your day in the country. The charming great house is festooned with thumbergia and replete with antiques.

A buffet lunch is highlighted by roast suckling pig chosen from the piggery at the rear. Horse rides are available. *For information contact: Hilton High, PO Box 162, Reading, Montego Bay. Tel: (876) 952 3343;*

Superb yachting cruises are one of the major draws of the Caribbean, and Jamaica is no exception

www.jamaicahiltontour.com.
Open: daily 8am–3pm.

National Parks

The National Environment and Planning Agency (NEPA, *10–11 Caledonia Ave, Kingston 5. Tel: (876) 754 7540; www.nepa.gov.jm*) protects the island's natural resources.

Creation of the **Montego Bay Marine Park** in 1990 reflects the commitment to environment conservation. The sanctuary safeguards the shore and coastal waters from the Donald Sangster International Airport to the Great River. Water sports are available in designated areas. The **Blue Mountains and John Crow National Park** protects 79,127 hectares (195,527 acres) of endangered forest habitat. The **Negril Watershed Park** protects vital wetland habitats. The **Cockpit Country**, **Hellshire Hills** and **Black River Great Morass** are among six other areas to be protected. **Ghourie State Park** has many woodland trails. Spelunking is possible inside Ghourie Caves.

A very useful source of information is the **Jamaica Environment Trust** (*58 Half Way Tree Rd, Kingston 10; tel: (876) 960 3693; www.jamentrust.org*).

Sailing trips

Choose from a plethora of yachting cruises available in major tourist areas. Most of the larger resorts have their own resident day-trip boats.

Alternatively, brochures and pamphlets on who is offering what will certainly be on display at any hotel's reception desk.

In Montego Bay, **MoBay Undersea Tours** (*tel: (876) 940 4465; www.mobayunderseatours.com*) operates a semi-sub vessel which sinks below the waves for a great view of the coral reef and its fish. Tours run twice daily except Wednesdays. The company also owns *Calico*, a 17m (55ft) wooden ketch that sets sail every morning and evening, in time to catch the sunrise and sunset. From Doctor's Cave Beach a well-kept catamaran, *Tropical Dreamer* (*tel: (876) 979 0102*), cruises along the coast to Margaritaville and stops for snorkelling along the way.

In Ocho Rios options include similar catamaran cruises organised from its main beach by **Heave-Ho** (*tel: (876) 974 5367; www.heaveho.net*) and *Cool Runnings* (*tel: (876) 974 4593; www.fivestarwatersports.com*). Heave-Ho occasionally runs weekend trips to Cuba.

In Negril, boat trips run straight along the coast from Long Bay but also to Half Moon Bay, a lovely private beach, for picnics. Operators include **Red Stripe** (*tel: (876) 640 0873*) and **Wild Thing** (*tel: (876) 957 5392*). A more unusual tour is the **Jamaica Rhino Safari** (*tel: (876) 877 0781; www.jamaicarhinosafaris.com*), which gives visitors the chance to power their own inflatable craft through mangrove swamps and out to sea.

River rafting

A leisurely raft trip is guaranteed to add romance to any Jamaica holiday. Swashbuckling film hero Errol Flynn is credited with initiating rafting on the Rio Grande as a fun-filled tourist attraction. The sport was later encouraged by the Earl of Mansfield, who built a restaurant and pavilion at Rafter's Rest, the terminal of the journey once made by banana boatmen. Today, rafting is a well-established, well-organised attraction.

Rafting trips are offered on the Rio Grande in Port Antonio, the White River near Ocho Rios, and the Great and Martha Brae rivers near Montego Bay. The journey is like drifting through Shangri-La. Each river threads

Bamboo poles tied together may seem a precarious form of transport but rafts are professionally steered and a lovely way to see the scenery

The rafting roster

A bar-raft may sidle up beside you to offer to sell you a rum punch, a beer or tourist trinkets (even on the river, the hagglers are present). Cattle graze the margins, while egrets and herons stand silently fishing for freshwater shrimp. You may even round a bend to be greeted by a band that will break into a calypso tune for your benefit.

The best rafting is the 10km (6-mile), 2½-hour journey down the Rio Grande. The trip begins at either Grants Level or Berridale, from where you drift to the river mouth at Rafter's Rest. Your car will have been driven to Rafter's Rest to await you. For information contact: Rio Grande Attractions, PO Box 128, Port Antonio; *tel: (876) 993 5778*.

Shorter trips on the Martha Brae (Martha Brae Rafting; *tel: (876) 952 0889*) and Great River (Mountain Valley Rafting; *tel: (876) 956 4920*) offer a one-hour glide. They begin at Rafter's Village, south of Falmouth, and Lethe, where beds are available, respectively. The Great River trip includes a midday stop at a scenic recreation area, where you can enjoy donkey rides and laze in a hammock, drinking coconut water or your favourite cocktail. The White River trip takes 45 minutes, including a short swimming stop at Calypso Cove (Calypso Rafting; *tel: (876) 974 2527; www.calypsorafting.com*).

down through green mountains, with trees arching overhead and vaulting cliffs that occasionally fall dark to the water.

Your transport is a long, narrow bamboo raft with a raised double seat, about two-thirds of the way back. You are propelled by the gentle flow and a stout bamboo pole deftly wielded by the licensed raftsman, who stands near the front with water washing his feet. Sometimes the water is shallow, clear and green and mountain pure. At other times it is deep and you may swim next to the raft in deep, cool pools.

Shopping

Jamaica offers much for those who like to strike a bargain, be it a duty-free camera, hand-rolled cigars, an almost nonexistent bikini, a woodcarving or a fine piece of art hardwon from a 'higgler'.

Islandwide there are craft stalls and marketplaces where you can try your hand at the Jamaican sport of higgling (*see pp146–7*). Never pay the asking price, except in formal establishments.

The island also boasts many shopping centres, where you can find everything from pottery to electronics.

Do not be lured to particular stores by hired drivers or guides who often receive commissions.

Jamaica has a general consumption tax (GCT) of 16.5 per cent, which is added to all purchases at point of sale.

Clothing

Jamaica has a handful of fashionable designers producing stylish daywear and elegant evening outfits. One of the most successful is Cedella Marley, daughter of Bob, who has a small shop selling her Catch A Fire range at the Bob Marley Museum in Kingston.

Ubiquitous T-shirts tout the virtues of reggae and *ganja* (marijuana). Cooyah and 2000lb are Jamaican T-shirt brands with quality products and classier designs.

Duty-free shops

Jamaica is brimful of duty-free shops selling 'in-bond' china, crystal, watches, perfume and designer leather goods. Savings run from 10 to 40 per cent. Check prices at home beforehand. In-bond items must be purchased in foreign currency and picked up at airports or piers as you leave. You can also buy at duty-free stores in the airport departure lounges. However, you must produce an airline ticket and identification.

Souvenirs

The government-sponsored Things Jamaican shops offer the finest crafts. Craft markets tend towards straw goods, woodcarvings, shell craft, hammocks and T-shirts. Quality varies. Many are first-rate and make evocative mementoes.

There is plenty of jewellery, both trinket and designer variety. Beware so-called 'gold' jewellery. It may be fake. Avoid black coral, shell, crocodile and tortoiseshell items – they are illegal!

Don't leave without some delectable Blue Mountain coffee, world-famous Appleton rum, or some Fiery Jerk Seasoning from Walkerswood.

KINGSTON
Devon House
The home of Things Jamaican. Shops sell everything from T-shirts to paintings, coffee and rum.
26 Hope Rd. Tel: (876) 929 6602.
Open: Mon–Sat 10am–6pm.
New Kingston Shopping Centre
A chic mall with 37 shops including fashion boutiques.
30 Dominica Drive, New Kingston.
Open: Mon–Sat 10am–6pm.
Tropical Plaza
This popular 16-store shopping area offers everything most tourists could want, at competitive prices.
134 Constant Spring Rd.
Open: Mon–Sat 9am–6pm.
Frame Centre Gallery
A wonderful collection of fine art.
10 Tangerine Place, Kingston.
Tel: (876) 926 4644.

THE WEST
Mo'Bay's main shopping village complexes are at the downtown City Centre Mall and Half Moon Village.

Negril's best shopping plaza is Times Square on Norman Manley Boulevard.
Bob Marley Experience
This shop boasts the largest collection of Bob Marley T-shirts in the world.
Half Moon Village, Montego Bay.
Gallery of West Indian Art
A showcase of fine Jamaican art.
11 Fairfield Rd, Catherine Hall.
Tel: (876) 052 4547;
www.galleryofwestindianart.com
Kuyaba
A small souvenir shop with decently made and attractive crafts.
Kuyaba Hotel, Negril.
Tel: (876) 957 4318.

NORTH COAST
Ocho Rios has three crafts markets – the best is the small Olde Craft Market – and several duty-free malls. Island Village is the most attractive shopping plaza, with good book and CD shops and its own beach.
Gallery Joe James
Naïve paintings, carvings and masks.
Hotel Rio Bueno, Rio Bueno.
Tel: (876) 954 0046.
Wassi Art
Ceramic art studio where visitors can watch dishes being made.
Great Pond, near Fern Gully. Tel: (876) 974 5044; www.wassiart.com

THE EAST
Lioness
African wraps, dresses and jewellery, and hand-made drums.
10 Matthews Ave. Tel: (876) 715 3529.
Things Jamaican
Superb Jamaican crafts and foodstuffs.
Port Antonio Marina.
Tel: (876) 715 5247.

Markets

'Can I sell you sometin' sweet, darlin'?' calls a jubilant woman in colourful garb. Carrots, shallots, beets, grapefruit, mangoes and sugar cane stripped down to its juicy core are spread out in brilliant display. You are surrounded by a whirligig of petty trading. Welcome to a public market – a fairground of colour and sound – where 'higglers' (street pedlars) hawk their wares.

Every town has a public market, best visited late in the week, when the activity is more intense. The scene generally looks like a little piece of Africa. The open-air markets abound in yams and turnips, lima-bean-like gungo peas, squash and pumpkins, breadfruit and ackee, garlic and onions, and tiny red, fiery peppers.

'Market Mammies' are queens of the trade. Their uniform is a 'bib', a large apron, with two deep pockets designed to foil pickpockets. They keep most of their money safe in cloth 'threadbags' buried deep in their bosoms, along with garlic or grains of corn as charms against thieves. You, too, should stay alert about your personal items.

Uniquely Jamaican markets such as Papine, at the east end of Hope Road, are scattered throughout Kingston. Go with a local guide. Coronation Market, the island's largest market, overflows North and South Parade. Wooden handcarts and rickety wooden stalls are stacked high with produce, mountains of brassieres, and even scrap salvaged from the local corporation dump or 'dungle'.

The Montego Bay Public Market is on Fustic Street. In Port Antonio, check out Musgrave Market, a great place to purchase Blue Mountain coffee, eye-catching leatherwork,

Rasta hats on sale

Fresh fruit and vegetables for sale in the market

tropical flower perfumes and a wide range of touristy souvenirs.

Every resort has a lively craft market for tourists. Offerings run from handwoven baskets, straw hats and Jamaica-shaped key chains to etched calabash gourds, jazzy T-shirts and hammocks.

Mo'Bay's Crafts Market, on Howard Cook Boulevard at Fort Street, is one of the largest. Nearby is the Old Fort Craft Park, behind the fort on Gloucester Avenue. Vendors are licensed by the Jamaica Tourist Board.

The straw market at Ocean Village in Ocho Rios offers a special bounty of straw hats, place mats, rugs and the like. The items are made here from palm fronds or the straw of jipijapa, the plant of which Panama hats are made. The best bargains are found after cruise passengers have returned to their ships. Woodcarving stalls atop Dunn's River Falls display creations in mahogany, ebony and lignum vitae (a rose-coloured hardwood).

The Negril Crafts Park, at the junction of Norman Manley Boulevard and West End Road, is terrific for wooden carvings and T-shirts. Kingston's Victoria Crafts Market, Port Royal Street near Victoria Pier, is less expensive than more touristy markets.

Most craft markets are open Monday to Friday 8am–5pm and Saturdays 8am–6pm.

Entertainment

Tame by day, Jamaica 'gets down' by night. From reggae to opera, the options are many. There are nightclubs, of course, and frequent one-off parties, known as bashments or jump-ups and usually held outdoors. Most larger hotels have nightly floor shows to keep guests amused. This tends towards limbo and Carnival-style 'junkanoo' dancers, live calypso bands and Caribbean theme parties.

When you have had your fill of theme nights, throw on your T-shirt and get ready to jam at any of hundreds of discos nationwide. Many larger hotels have their own nightclubs, where non-guests are welcome. Even the most remote village has its 'disco', which may be just a set of speakers (usually of unbelievable size) tied to a tree.

In Kingston and, to a much lesser extent, Mo'Bay, outside parties keep the party going – the streets vibrate with DeeJay music, *ganja* (marijuana) smoke hangs thick in the air, and you will dance shoulder-to-sweaty-shoulder with a mostly Jamaican crowd. Where you land depends on what night it is. Leave jewellery and purses in your hotel safety-deposit box.

Kingston is Jamaica's cultural centre, with a lively tradition of performing arts, including classical symphony, choral, folk music, and classical and contemporary dance. Kingston, too, is famous for its lively pantomime season, when satirical vignettes spoof current affairs.

Jamaica hosts many festivals of world renown. Every summer, it hosts one of the largest music gatherings in the world: Reggae Sumfest, in Montego Bay.

Sunset is absolutely free. In Negril it is almost a religious experience, and tourists flock nightly like lemmings to Rick's Cafe to watch the sun slide from view.

The Jamaica Tourist Board publishes a *Calendar of Events* on its website and can provide information on up-to-date happenings. There are several other websites dedicated to events listings in Jamaica: *www.whatsonjamaica.com*, *www.whaddat.com*, *www.jamaicanlifestyle.com*. Otherwise, radio stations and newspapers – especially *The Daily Gleaner* – are good sources of information. The locals rely on banners, posters and flyers to keep abreast of forthcoming events.

Beach parties

Jamaicans excel at beach parties, sometimes known as *boonoonoonoos*, a patois word meaning 'great'. These vary from well-organised family affairs to bacchanals with virtual X-rated dancing! Live reggae music, plus open bar and buffet dinner are staples. A cover charge applies and though these are mostly one-off occasions they always take place at the weekends and there are regular venues:

Dead End Beach,
Montego Bay
Fort Clarence Beach,
Kingston
James Bond Beach,
Oracabessa
Reggae Beach, Ocho Rios
Walter Fletcher Beach,
Montego Bay
Shanshay Beach, Port
Antonio
Winnifred Beach, Port
Antonio

Check the press for details of upcoming beach parties. Flyers will be posted all over the relevant town!

Cinemas

Carib 5 Cinema
Cross Roads, Kingston.
Tel: (876) 906 1090.

The Cove
Island Village, Ocho Rios.
Tel: (876) 675 8902.
Diamond Cinema
Ironshore, Montego Bay.
Tel (876) 953 9540.
Island Cinemax
Island Life Centre,
Kingston.
Tel: (876) 920 7964.
Caledonia Ave,
Mandeville.
Tel: (876) 962 1354.
Palace Cineplex
106 Hope Rd, Kingston.
Tel: (876) 978 8286.
Palace Multiplex
Alice Eldemire Drive,
Montego Bay.
Tel: (876) 971 5550.

Classical music
The **Jamaica Philharmonic Symphony Orchestra** and **National Chorale Orchestra** perform at Kingston's Little Theatre, 4 Tom Redcam Avenue (*tel: (876) 926 6129*) and other venues.
The **Philip Sherlock Centre for Creative Arts** (*tel: (876) 927 1660*) at the University of the West Indies at Mona hosts classical, popular and folklore performances by the University Singers.

Dance
The National Dance Theatre Company (*tel: (876) 926 6129*) performs its Season of Dance at the Little Theatre, July–August and December. L'Acadco (L'Antoinette Caribbean American Dance Company) *tel: (876) 938 2039; www.lacadco.org*), is a modern-dance company which takes its inspiration from African folklore.

Jazz
Jazz comes to Jamaica every June with an annual jazz festival in Ocho Rios that attracts big-name performers (*see p21*).
Bluebeat Jazz and Blues Bar
Live jazz and blues nightly.
Tel: (876) 952 4777.
Gloucester Ave,
Montego Bay.
Christopher's Jazz Café
Live jazz several nights a week.
20–22 Trinidad Terrace,
Kingston.
Tel: (876) 754 8723.
Pool Bar, Hilton Hotel
Live jazz on Sunday evenings.

77 Knutsford Blvd,
Kingston.
Tel: (876) 926 5430.

**Polo Grounds Bar,
Coyaba Hotel**
Live jazz on Friday
evenings.
Ironshore, Montego Bay.
Tel: (876) 953 9150.

Red Bones Café
Live jazz and blues bands
occasionally.
21 Braemar Rd, Kingston.
Tel: (876) 978 8262.

Karaoke

Jamaicans love karaoke
and many bars have a
weekly karaoke session.
Performances are
surprisingly professional
and there are often
queues of singers waiting
to take their turn.

The Brewery
Miranda Ridge,
Montego Bay.
Tel: (876) 979 2613.

Coral Cliffs
Gloucester Ave,
Montego Bay.
Tel: (876) 952 4130.

Indies
8 Holborn Rd, Kingston.
Tel: (876) 926 2952.

Mingles
Courtleigh Hotel,
Kingston.
Tel: (876) 929 9000.

Mo'Bay Proper
Fort St, Montego Bay.
Tel: (876) 940 1233.

Nightclubs

There are nightclubs in
most towns in Jamaica.
Many stay open all night
– it's rare for Jamaicans
to come home before
dawn. Jamaica's in-vogue
dance styles are typified
by *wine on ah bumsee*,
which roughly translates
as 'to make sexual
motions on a woman's
behind'. Many local
nightclubs feature
dancers performing
risqué acts.

KINGSTON

Asylum
69 Knutsford Blvd.
Tel: (876) 929 4386.

Jonkanoo Lounge
Hilton Kingston,
77 Knutsford Blvd.
Tel: (876) 926 5430.

Mingles
Courtleigh Hotel,
Knutsford Blvd.
Tel: (876) 929 9000.

Peppers
31 Upper Waterloo Rd.
Tel: (876) 969 2421.

Quad
20–22 Trinidad Terrace.
Tel: (876) 754 7823.

Weekendz
80 Constant Spring Rd.
Tel: (876) 755 4415.

MONTEGO BAY

Hurricanes
Breezes resort,
Gloucester Ave.
Tel: (876) 940 1150.

Margaritaville
Gloucester Ave.
Tel: (876) 952 4777.

Mo'Bay Proper
44 Fort St.
Tel: (876) 940 1235.

Pier One
Howard Cooke Blvd.
Tel: (876) 952 2452.

Voyage
Walter Fletcher Beach.
Tel: (876) 940 1344.

MANDEVILLE

Jerky's
Winston Jones
Highway.

The Link
80 Caledonia Ave.
Tel: (876) 962 3771.

NEGRIL

The Jungle
Norman Manley Blvd.
Tel: (876) 957 4005.

OCHO RIOS

Amnesia
70 Main St.
Tel: (876) 974 2633.

Jamaica'N Me Crazy
Sunset Jamaican Grande Hotel, Main St.
Tel: (876) 974 2200.
The Cage
White River.
Tel: (876) 795 3539.

PORT ANTONIO
Roof Club
11 West St.
Tel: (876) 993 2127.
Shadows
40 West St.
Tel: (876) 993 3823.

RUNAWAY BAY
Safari Disco
Club Ambiance Resort.
Tel: (876) 973 6167.

Oldies nights
Oldies nights are weekly music events held in clubs all over the island, with the best of vintage Jamaican ska and rocksteady music. It's common to see old men in pork-pie hats and suits grooving away into the small hours.
Pier Lounge
21 West Palm Ave, Port Antonio.
Priscillas
109 Constant Spring Rd, Kingston.
Tel: (876) 969 9638.

Randles
Hart St, Montego Bay.

Piano bars and pubs
Glenn's Cocktail Lounge
Tower Isle, Ocho Rios.
Tel: (876) 975 4360.
Jamaica Pegasus Hotel
81 Knutsford Blvd, Kingston.
Tel: (876) 926 3690.
Mandeville Arms
Mandeville Hotel, Mandeville.
Tel: (876) 962 9764.
Richmond Hill Inn
Richmond Hill, Montego Bay.
Tel: (876) 952 3859.

Reggae concerts and stageshows
You are sure to find one or more groups playing at weekend beach parties all over the island, and many of Jamaica's nightclubs play host to live performances. Negril has a handful of bars on its beach with live music most nights a week. The most popular are:
Alfred's Ocean Palace
Tel: (876) 957 4735.
Bourbon Beach Bar
Tel: (876) 957 4405.
Roots Bamboo
Tel: (876) 957 4479.

Outdoors stageshows are huge events in Jamaica. They rarely start before midnight and if it rains they're always called off. Listed are some of the best annual stageshows on the island (you'll need to check the press for exact details since they move both venue and dates from year to year):
Heineken Startime
Year-round. Kingston.
Rebel Salute
January. Kaiser Sports Club, St Elizabeth.
Saddle in the East
Goodyear Oval, St Thomas.
Western Consciousness
April. Savanna-la-Mar.

Theatre
Kingston has a flourishing drama scene.
The Barn
5 Oxford Rd. Tel: (876) 926 6469.
Little Theatre
4 Tom Redcam Ave, Kingston.
Tel: (876) 926 6129.
New Kingston Theatre
Altamont Crescent.
Tel: (876) 929 2618.
Ward Theatre
North Parade, Kingston.
Tel: (876) 922 0453.

Sumfest

For several days every summer, Jamaica holds an event that commands the world music stage. Legions of reggae fans flock from every corner of the globe. Hotels sell out. And 100,000 joyous revellers dance beneath the stars to the syncopated rhythms of the world's most irresistible beat.

When Reggae Sunsplash, once the world's premier reggae showcase, ran

The Skatalites, going strong since 1964

into administrative and financial difficulties in the late 1990s, the younger Reggae Sumfest took up the reins. Established in 1993 and, like Sunsplash, based in Montego Bay, Sumfest has become a huge annual event on the live-music calender.

In recent years artists such as 50 Cent, Missy Elliot and Destiny's Child have performed at Sumfest as well as home-grown talent Buju Banton, Lady Saw and Bounty Killer.

Like Sunsplash, Sumfest's multi-day – and night – festival keeps the masses dancing and swaying until the sun rises above the calm Caribbean. Clouds of *ganja* (marijuana) swirl above the crowd. And the sensation of 'one love' – the creed of racial harmony coined by the late reggae legend Bob Marley – is palpable as the trouble-free crowd undulates, hip-to-hip, to the sensual dawn-to-dusk orgy of music.

Variants of the familiar reggae beat are presented on themed evenings. Past Sumfests have included Danceclass, Dancehall Night, Reggae Night and International Night. The best examples of each genre are invited to attend, ranging from the latest exponents of the medium to more established and better known performers, such as Burning Spear, Third World, Toots and the Maytals, Ziggy Marley and Shabba Ranks. *For further information contact: www.reggaesumfest.com*

If you go, wear loose, lightweight clothing and comfortable shoes. Otherwise you cannot 'ride de riddims'. Take a sweater or jacket in case the night turns cool. A cushion, stool or mat is useful. Sleep through the preceding afternoon.

In 2006 Reggae Sunsplash returned in a brand-new venue near the north-coast community of Priory in St Anns. With new life pumped into it and veteran performers such as Gregory Isaacs, Maxi Priest and Steel Pulse as well as Damian Marley and Elephant Man, it seems that the older festival may be back to compete with Sumfest. *For further information contact: www.reggaesunsplashja.com*

Reggae Sunsplash

Children

Jamaicans adore children. There are several good amusement parks on the island which have a variety of activities for the young. Climbing waterfalls, horse-riding and snorkelling are also popular with older children. Supermarkets islandwide stock baby milk, children's food and nappies (diapers). The JTB website (www. visitjamaica.com) has all kinds of information about family holidays and attractions suitable for children.

Animal Farm

Animal Farm has a collection of exotic birds and snakes, a petting zoo and trails explaining the use of various Jamaican plants. There are donkey-rides and friendly guides who cater their tours to appeal to children.
Close to Lethe in St James' interior. Tel: (876) 815 4104. Open: Mon–Fri by appointment only, Sat & Sun 10am–5pm. Admission charge.

Beaches

Bring a bucket and spade – your children will want to spend countless hours on the beach. The calm, shallow waters are perfect for children. Pedal-boats and other water sports, including children's snorkelling equipment, are widely available.

Hotels

Many hotels welcome children and have play directors and supervised activities. Children under 6 generally stay free when overnighting with parents.

Occasionally those aged 6–15 are charged a much reduced rate – otherwise they also stay free.

Or consider a villa, which gives you absolute freedom and may prove most cost-effective for large families.

Beaches is the award-winning family-friendly offshoot of couples-only specialist Sandals and has three resorts in Jamaica: **Beaches Negril** (tel: (876) 957 9270), **Beaches Sandy Bay** (tel: (876) 957 5100) and **Beaches Boscobel** (tel: (876) 975 7777), close to Ocho Rios (www.beaches.com).

There are toddler pools, petting zoos, magic shows and every possible facility for children, including X-Box game centres for bored teenagers. There are even life-sized Sesame Street characters wandering the hotel grounds and entertaining the children with activities like singing or cooking.

Franklyn D Resorts

There are two FDR resorts on the island: the original Franklyn D Resort

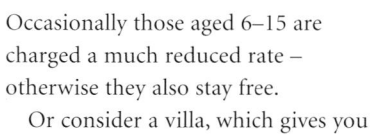

in Runaway Bay (*tel: (876) 973 4591*) and Pebbles in Falmouth (*tel: (876) 973 4591*). Both hotels have a full range of water sports, a Yellow Bird Kids' club, toddlers' wading pool and a Teen Centre with rap sessions and karaoke. (*www.fdrholidays.com*)

Starfish

Starfish Trelawny is situated near Falmouth and has all kinds of kid-friendly features. These include four swimming pools, a 38m (124ft) waterslide and a flying trapeze. (*Tel: 925 0925; www.starfishresorts.com*)

Falmouth Swamp Safari

Crocodile feeding time is sure to keep children rapt. The park has a petting zoo and bird sanctuary, plus snakes and mongooses as well as a breeding centre. *3km (2 miles) west of Falmouth. Tel: (876) 954 3065. Open: daily 8.30am–5pm (guided tours available). Admission charge.*

Kool Runnings

Negril's newest attraction is a state-of-the-art water park with seven huge slides – the longest, Yellow Constrictor (named after Jamaica's biggest snake), is 107m (350ft) long. There's a man-made river complete with waterfalls, an activities centre with kids' games and all kinds of food options. *Situated near Sandals on Norman Manley Blvd. Tel: (876) 957 5400; www.koolrunnings.com. Open: daily 9am–6pm. Admission charge.*

White River Valley

Children will love the adrenalin-fuelled activities such as river-tubing, kayaking and horse riding. Adults might enjoy the more sedate nature trails and attractive cafés! *Situated in the St Mary's interior, near Ocho Rios. Tel: (876) 917 337. www.wrvja.com. Open daily 9am–5pm. Admission charge.*

Meeting local children

The Jamaican Tourist Board's Meet the People programme (*see p27*) will match you with a family of similar ages and interests. Alternatively, you can contact Countrystyle International (*tel: (876) 962 7758/488 7207; www. countrystylecommunitytourism.com*), which can also match you with a family for overnight stays.

Smartly dressed school children

Children

Sport and leisure

Jamaica's realm of sports takes some beating, whether on or under land or in, on or under water. While you may be astonished to learn that Jamaica has an Olympic bobsleigh team, this is one of the few activities you will not find offered. (You can, however, take tours with the dogs that form part of the Jamaica dog-sled team! Contact Chukka Caribbean for details; www.chukkacaribbean.com*)*

The possibilities will exhaust you, whether you choose an invigorating horse ride, a tennis grand slam, or a round of golf in the footsteps of the pros. Water sports include sailing, game fishing, windsurfing and waterskiing. And you can slip on your snorkel or scuba gear and discover a Jamaica that is as beautiful below as it is above.

Major resort hotels offer sports fitness centres. Negril's 4ha (10-acre) **Couples Swept Away** (*tel: (876) 957 4061; www.swept-away.com*) is the most comprehensive, with ten floodlit tennis courts, a 25m (82ft) swimming pool, an aerobics centre, air-conditioned squash, racquetball and basketball courts, and a jogging path centred in and around the Sports and Fitness Complex. It is open to the public for a small fee.

Spectator sports include cricket (*see pp162–3*) and football which has grown hugely in popularity since the national team, known as the Reggae Boyz, qualified for the World Cup in 1998. Matches are noisy events complete with ear-splitting interval music and fanatic support.

Boating

Most resorts offer Sunfish or Sailfish – small boats ideal for playing around in close to shore. Larger boats may be chartered from yacht clubs in Kingston, Montego Bay, Port Antonio and Port Royal. Make sure operators are licensed by the Jamaica Tourist Board. For information contact the **Royal Jamaica Yacht Club** (*tel: (876) 924 8685; www.rjyc.prg.jm*) in Kingston; **Morgan's Harbour Marina** (*tel: (876) 967 8040; www.morgansharbour.com*) in Port Royal; or the **Montego Bay Yacht Club** (*tel: (876) 979 8038; www.montego-bay-jamaica.com*). In Port Antonio, boat rentals are available through **Port Antonio Marina** (*tel: (876) 927 0145; www.errolflynnmarina.com*).

Game fishing

Beyond the reefs, Jamaica's waters are a marine paradise. Beginning as close as a

2km (1¹/₂ miles) offshore, the ocean floor plummets to immeasurable depths, marking the edge of the Cayman Trench, the deepest region in the entire Caribbean. Known as Marlin Alley, it is a migratory path for prized blue marlin and other deepwater game fish – yellowfin tuna, wahoo, kingfish and barracuda – that run through these waters year-round.

Jamaica hosts several blue marlin tournaments, topped by the annual International Marlin Tournament of Port Antonio. The best time for marlin is September to April, with prize catches usually caught between June and August.

Jamaica boasts three primary fishing centres: Negril, Port Antonio and Montego Bay. Half- and full-day charters can be booked through most major hotels. No licences are required. Most boats accommodate up to six passengers. Most skippers expect a 50 per cent deposit and 24 hours' advance reservation. Book only through the skipper or crew member, never with bystanders on the dock. Charter boats usually keep 50 per cent of the catch.

Golf

Jamaica is blessed with rippling green fairways that border the blue Caribbean. Golf is Jamaica's great sporting strength. It has more courses than any other Caribbean island. Booking ahead is essential. Carts are available at most courses, as are caddies, who carry golf bags on their heads!

Jamaica's first course was established in the mid-1800s at Mandeville. It is a quaint 9-hole course with 18 tee positions, located at the **Manchester Club** (*tel: (876) 962 2403*), 670m (2,200ft) high in the cool mountains.

The **Tryall Golf, Tennis and Beach Club** (*tel: (876) 956 5660; www.tryallclub.com*) is irrefutably the island's best course. The 6,328m (6,920yd), par-71 course is contoured on the site of an 18th-century sugar plantation. Tryall is an official PGA Tour approved course.

There are four excellent golf courses in Ironshore, near Montego Bay, making it Jamaica's golf capital.

Rose Hall resort (*tel: (876) 953 2650; www.rosehallresort.com*), east of Montego Bay, is the venue for the PGA-sanctioned Jamaica Open. The prevailing winds and severe doglegs challenge even the most accomplished golfer. The 6,218m (6,800yd), par-72 course has magnificent sea views.

The **Ritz-Carlton's White Witch Golf Course** (*tel: (876) 518 0174; www.ritzcarlton.com*), also east of Montego Bay, is one of the finest courses in the world. Built on over 240 hectares (600 acres) of rolling countryside, 16 of the 18 holes offer spectacular views over the sea.

Ironshore (*tel: (876) 953 2800*) is a 6,008m (6,570yd), par-72, links-type course.

The Robert Trent Jones-designed championship course (6,510m/

7,119yds, par-72) is at the **Half Moon** resort (*tel: (876) 953 3105; www.halfmoongolf.com*).

Ocho Rios also boasts two courses: **Sandals Golf and Country Club** (*tel: (876) 975 0119; www.sandals.com*) is owned by the Sandals resort chain. The 18-hole course (6,035m/6,600yd), par-71), formerly Upton Golf Club, is free to guests at any of Sandals' six properties.

The **Superclubs Golf Course** (*tel: (876) 973 7319; www.superclubs.com*) at Runaway Bay in Ocho Rios is another superb challenge (6,282m/6,870yds, par-72). It hosts the annual Superclubs Golf Invitational tournament in September.

The **Negril Hills Golf Club** (*tel: (876) 957 4638; www.negrilhillsgolfclub.com*), with rippling fairways overlooking the Great Morass, has plenty of water hazards, including crocodile-infested wetlands.

Kingston has two courses: **Caymanas** (*tel: (876) 922 3386; www.caymanasgolfclub.com*), Jamaica's first 18-hole championship course, and **Constant Spring** (*tel: (876) 922 3388*).

Green fees range from JM$1,600–3,500. Clubs can be rented for about JM$12–35 a round.

There are two state-of-the-art golf schools in Jamaica, both on Mo'Bay – at Half Moon and the Ritz-Carlton. *For further information contact the Jamaica Golf Association (tel: (876) 906 7636; www.jamaicagolfassociation.com).*

Horse riding

Stables throughout the island offer everything from polo matches to pony treks that guarantee a relaxing means of exploring offbeat Jamaica. Options range from canters along the coast to rugged rides into the mountains. Most hotels can arrange horse riding through local stables.

Chukka Cove in St Ann's Bay is the home of the **St Ann's Bay Polo Club** and the original location for tour operator Chukka Caribbean (*www.chukkacaribbean.com*). They still offer their original ride 'n' swim trek along the coast.

Also in St Ann's Bay are horse-tour specialists **Hooves** (*tel: (876) 972 0905; www.hoovesjamaica.com*) who take groups through the Seville Great House and Heritage Park, along rivers and down to the sea.

The Half Moon Equestrian Centre (*tel: (876) 953 2268; www. horsebackridingjamaica.com*) at the Half Moon Resort in Montego Bay is the best riding school on the island with thoroughbred horses and lessons in polo, dressage and show-jumping as well as popular beach treks.

The **Rocky Point Stables** (*tel: (876) 953 2286*) at the Half Moon Club, Montego Bay, also offers trail rides and riding lessons. At **Good Hope** (*tel: (876) 469 3443; www. goodhopejamaica.com*), near Falmouth, guests can canter through orchards of coconut, papaya and ugli; then dive into the Martha Brae and follow the stream-side bridle path back to the old plantation.

In Ocho Rios there is horse riding available at the **Prospect Plantation** (*tel: (876) 994 1508*) and the White River Valley leisure park (*tel: (876) 917 3373; www.wrvja.com*). Also on the north coast, the **Braco Stables** (*tel: (876) 954 0185; www.bracostables.com*) has horse-riding tours through the grounds of a large estate.

In Negril, check with **Rhodes Hall Plantation** (*tel: (876) 957 6883; www.rhodeshallresort.com*) which offers two-hour rides through the estate and along the beach.

Horse racing

If you want to lay odds on a winner, horse racing takes place every Wednesday, Saturday and public holidays at **Caymanas Park** (*tel: (876) 988 2523; www.caymanaspark.com*), near Kingston.

Parasailing

You 'fly' beneath a parachute attached to a speedboat churning along 30m (100ft) below your dangling legs. If man had wings, it would be like this! Trips last 20 to 30 minutes and can be booked through water-sport concessions at every major beach resort.

Scuba diving

Jamaica's shoreline waters quickly change from turquoise to royal blue to deep indigo. A single reef runs along the entire north coast. Water temperature averages 24°C (75°F), with visibility ranging from 21 to 36.5m (70 to 120ft).

If you've got all the gear, you can scuba dive at St Ann's Bay

Dozens of resorts and diving operators cater for the experienced diver. Novices can easily gain SCUBA certification, while those already certified will find tanks widely available for hire. You must show a certification card to rent scuba gear or participate in guided diving trips.

Montego Bay is famous for its wall dives. Old Airport Reef is considered the best site on the island, known for its coral caves, tunnels and canyons. Jacques Cousteau marvelled at its 'dramatic sponge life'. Local companies include **Captain's Watersports and Dive Centre** (*tel: (876) 956 7312; www.captainsdivecenter.com*), **Dive Seaworld** (*tel: (876) 953 2180*) and **Resort Divers** (*tel: (876) 953 9699; www.resortdivers.com*). Between St Ann's Bay and Ocho Rios, the wall is within swimming distance of shore and there are numerous dive sites in the area, including sunken *ganja* planes and a Mercedes car.

Jamaqua at Club Ambiance, Runaway Bay (*tel: (876) 973 4845; www.jamaqua.com*) offers PADI certification and dive packages. Contact Garfield Diving Station (*tel: (876) 395 7023*) in Ocho Rios. In Port Antonio, **Lady G'Diver** (*tel: (876) 993 8988; www.ladygdiver.net*) is based at Port Antonio Marina and runs trips out to the Blue Lagoon. Kingston Harbour is one of the Caribbean's best-kept secrets; Port Royal has sunken ships that provide a haven for a dense array of tropical fish. Alas, no scuba-dive

SAVE THE REEFS!

It takes thousands of years for reefs to grow. Yet precious and fragile coral can be destroyed in a moment. The Negril Coral Reef Preservation Society issues the following cautions:

• Do not touch the coral. If you touch or stand on living coral it will die! Look… but don't touch!

• Do not litter the ocean. Rubbish is extremely harmful to marine life.

• Do not take or purchase black coral, conch shells, seafans, or starfish. It is illegal to take or purchase coral or tortoiseshell items.

• Do not molest or touch any marine life. Spearfishing is prohibited.

companies currently operate from Kingston.

Negril offers Treasure Reef, where spotted moray eels will pose for your camera. Try **Negril Scuba Centre** (*tel: (876) 957 4425; www.negrilscuba.com*) in the Mariner's Beach Club hotel. Other options include **Marine Life Divers** (*tel: (876) 957 9783; www.mldiversnegril.com*) and **Sun Divers** (*tel: (876) 957 4503; www.sundiversnegril.com*).

Spelunking

Jamaica is a spelunker's heaven. Almost two-thirds of the island is formed of limestone, much of it pockmarked with caves. The Cockpit Country and north central Jamaica are replete with cave systems. Options range from well-known 'show' caves like Windsor, Nonsuch and Two Sisters Caves, to hundreds of unexplored caves that will challenge the most intrepid spelunker.

Caves are poorly charted. Water levels can rise dramatically within minutes, and there is no cave rescue system. You enter at your own risk! Hire a guide, and ensure you are well prepared with flashlights and other necessary equipment.

Contact the **Jamaica Caves Organisation** (*www.jamaicancaves.org*), a highly professional outfit which offers advice and runs excellent caving tours.

Surfing

Jamaica is not noted as a surfer's paradise, although ripping waves are found on the east coast.

Boston Beach, 16km (10 miles) east of Port Antonio, has the biggest waves. You can rent boards here.

Tennis

Courts are abundant in all the resort areas, as well as Kingston and Mandeville. Every major hotel maintains tennis courts, many lighted for night-time play and many with resident pros. Non-guests can usually play for a fee. Rates for instruction vary.

Kingston boasts the **Eric Bell Tennis Centre**; it hosts the Jamaica International Tournament and is the home of Tennis Jamaica (*tel: (876) 978 1520; www.tennisjamaica.com*), formerly the Jamaica Lawn Tennis Association. In Montego Bay, the **Half Moon** resort (*www.halfmoon.com*) has 13 all-weather Laykold courts. Day passes are available to non-guests.

Windsurfing

Windsurfing is one of Jamaica's hottest water sports. Most beachfront hotels offer equipment, and instruction comes free for guests, or at a nominal price for non-guests. Most beaches have water-sports concession stands – their sales staff will come to you.

Waterskiing

Negril, with its 11km (7-mile) beach, is heaven for this. Many major hotels offer waterskiing free to guests. Even more popular is jet-skiing. Waterskis and jet-skis are available at water-sports concession stands and at hotels throughout the island.

The exciting sport of jet-skiing at Montego Bay

Cricket

Do not believe anyone who tells you that cricket is the sport of the English. Cricket truly belongs to the Caribbean. In Jamaica it comes close to a national mania. Michael Manley, the former prime minister, even wrote a lengthy book on the subject.

The popularity of cricket bears witness to Jamaica's strong British connections. The colonialists transplanted cricket throughout the British Empire and encouraged the game as part of a policy of breeding an affinity for the culture of the 'mother country'. In his book *Beyond a Boundary*, CL James claimed that one of the most comforting signs of Jamaica's readiness for self-rule was the island's zeal for the rules and sportsmanship of cricket.

The game, which in England gives way to soccer in winter, is a year-round sport in Jamaica. Round any corner or crest any hill, even in the

A cricket match at Sabina Park in Kingston

Any available patch of green is reason to establish a cricket pitch, where age is no barrier to one's eligibility to play. 'Cricket, lovely cricket!' Jamaicans are wild about it

most rural backwater, and you are likely to come across a village cricket match in progress, or youngsters practising their batting strokes and googlies with makeshift bat and ball.

When the English and Jamaican cricket teams meet at Kingston's Sabina Park, the whole island seems to erupt in excitement. The greatest triumph in the cricketing season is when Jamaica bests its former motherland – a result Jamaicans regard as taken for granted.

Jamaicans are masters of the idiosyncracies and subtleties that make cricket so complicated for foreigners to understand. The island has sired many of the world's finest cricketing impresarios: Alf Valetine, Lawrence Rowe and 'Collie' Smith.

The greatest of all Jamaican cricketing legends is George Headley, the modest cricketing genius born in Panama. He is Jamaica's 'Black Bradman', and during the 1920s and 1930s he averaged a test century every four innings. He remains the inspiration for thousands of youngsters for whom a distinguished cricketing career is an avenue for social advancement.

Cricket matches – 'curry goat' matches – between club teams are usually held at weekends. International and inter-island matches are normally held from January through to August at Kingston's Sabina Park, the grand shrine of cricket. Then, Sabina Park is packed to the gills, and families set up picnics. Enthusiastic roars wash down from the stands, where copious amounts of Jamaican rum and Red Stripe beer are imbibed.

Food and drink

Jamaica is a Garden of Eden of fresh produce, and cooking is one of the island's most joyful arts. Jamaica's uniquely zesty cuisine, a fusion of many ethnic traditions, offers a cornucopia of palate-tickling pleasures.

One of the pleasures of eating in Jamaica is dining on a terrace overlooking the sea. Another is sampling the spice-rich local cuisine. Most other international cuisines are represented, particularly in cosmopolitan Kingston. Food quality varies from bad to magnificent, and so do service and price, though not necessarily in direct correlation.

Virtually anywhere on the island you will pass by roadside stalls selling 'jerk' – pork, chicken or even lobster marinated in thyme, allspice and Scotch bonnet pepper and cooked over pimento wood so that the meat is saturated with flavour. You will never forget the first fiery morsel of jerk that detonates in your mouth!

Most Jamaican hotels offer guests a chance to taste local temptations such as mackerel 'run-down', escoveitched fish (marinated in vinegar, pepper and onions) served with festival bread, or curried goat, and ackee with codfish.

Basic roadside restaurants are atmospheric places to sample simple Jamaican dishes not found on most hotel menus: 'bammie', a toasted, pancake-flat spongy bread made from cassava; Mannish water, a soup (said to be an aphrodisiac) made from goats' heads and feet; and rice and peas (kidney beans), the island staple – often called the 'Jamaican Coat of Arms' – seasoned with onions and coconut milk.

You will also find plenty of restaurants that take pride in their white-glove service and romantic, candlelit ambience. Many of the best are in the de luxe hotels where imaginative chefs are introducing newly popular ingredients such as squash and fennel into Jamaican recipes dating back centuries. The result is a cross-cultural, home-grown Jamaican *nouvelle cuisine* that is emerging with pride.

If you simply *must* have fried chicken or a burger and chips, there are plenty of US-franchised fast-food places and local copies. Locally made hamburgers are usually spiced.

Vegetarians will be satisfied at one of several dozen Ital restaurants on the island. Ital food is eaten by Rastafarians, is meat-free and cooked without salt. Dishes are usually made up of steamed or fried vegetables – calalloo, pumpkin, ackee – served with spicy tofu or soya protein curries. Otherwise, Indian and Japanese restaurants all serve vegetarian options, as, increasingly, do many of the high-class places in our listings. All-inclusive resorts also provide a choice of dishes for vegetarians.

You can top off your meal with Blue Mountain coffee and maybe a smooth rum liqueur such as Tia Maria. Countless are the bars where you can enjoy hearty rum cocktails: perhaps a Humming bird or a Blue Mountain Cocktail or Zombie. Jamaica's favourite beer is Red Stripe, the local brew known as 'Jamaica's Policeman'.

In the restaurants recommended in the following pages, the star rating indicates the approximate cost for a three-course meal per person, excluding wine and other liquors.

★	under J$10
★★	from J$11 to J$17
★★★	from J$18 to J$25
★★★★	over J$25

KINGSTON

The capital city boasts restaurants from Lebanon to Korea, all run by Jamaicans. Some of the island's finest restaurants are here.

Akbar ★★★

The best Indian food in Kingston in an attractive air-conditioned room. The weekday lunchtime buffet is excellent value.
11 Holborn Rd, Kingston. Tel: (876) 926 3480.

Bob's Café ★★

Open-air café in the grounds of the Bob Marley Museum. Fresh juice and 'Ital' vegetarian dishes as well as imaginative meat and fish choices.
56 Hope Rd, Kingston. Tel: (876) 927 9152.

Preparing jerk chicken

Café What's On ★★

Tables inside and out with Jamaican breakfasts and international lunch selections – bagels, sandwiches, burritos and salads.

Devon House, 26 Hope Rd, Kingston.
Tel: (876) 929 4490.

Chelsea Jerk Centre ★

Down-to-earth local eatery, selling jerk chicken or pork in a big, sky-blue room. Bench seating.

7 Chelsea Ave, Kingston.
Tel: (876) 926 6322.

East ★★

Japanese restaurant with excellent sushi and sahimi as well as soups, tempura and noodles. Daily lunch specials.

Shop 51, Marketplace Mall, 67 Constant Spring Rd, Kingston.
Tel: (876) 960 3962.

Grog Shoppe ★★

Offers shady outdoor dining at historic Devon House. Food with a nouvelle Jamaican touch: ackee crepes, roast suckling pig and baked crab backs.

Devon House, 26 Hope Rd, Kingston.
Tel: (876) 960 9730.

Jade Garden ★★★★

Up-market locals choose this elegant and thoroughly contemporary restaurant for consistently good Chinese cuisine.

Sovereign Centre, 106 Hope Rd, Kingston.
Tel: (876) 978 3476.

Norma's on the Terrace ★★★★

Located at Devon House, here is the latest outlet for Jamaica's most famous chef, Norma Shirley. Local materials are presented to their best advantage.

Devon House, 26 Hope Rd, Kingston.
Tel: (876) 968 5488.

Prendy's ★★

Every Wednesday, Friday and Saturday, the Hellshire beach institution sets up in an outdoor setting. The best fried fish in Kingston comes to town. Also crab curries, steamed fish and lobster.

Putt 'n' Play, 75 Knutsford Blvd, Kingston.
Tel: (876) 881 9689.

Strawberry Hill ★★★★

The cognoscenti flock to this upscale mountain resort serving recherché nouvelle Jamaican dishes. And what views!

Irish Town, Blue Mountains.
Tel: (876) 944 8400.

Up on the Roof ★★★

Up-market Creole food in a stunning setting overlooking the city. Staples such as jerked food, curries and *roti* are given a new twist, and there are good vegetarian options also.

75 Knutsford Blvd, Kingston.
Tel: (876) 929 8033.

THE EAST

Barracuda ★★★

A sophisticated restaurant with attractive décor and a menu featuring all the Jamaican and international staples – steak, seafood and jerked meat.

1 Bridge St, Port Antonio.
Tel: (876) 715 6111.

Dickie's Best Kept Secret ★★★

Lurking within a roadside banana stall is one of the best restaurants in the area. Dickie, a chef trained at the area's finest hotel, presents his 5-course meals to the highest

standards. Reservations must be made at least several hours beforehand.
Bryan's Bay, Port Antonio. Tel: (876) 809 6276.

Dixon's Food Shop ★
Manna from heaven to vegetarians, this simple lunchtime joint has tofu dishes, salads and soups.
Bridge St, Port Antonio.

Norma's at the Marina ★★★★
The latest addition to chef Norma Shirley's stable of classy restaurants has outdoor tables on the small beach at the swanky Port Antonio Marina.
Port Antonio Marina. Tel: (876) 993 9510.

If you're just interested in a quick pitstop, Miss Shine-Eye's simple restaurant by Boundbrook Wharf has reputedly the best jerk chicken in Jamaica. Jerk barbecues on the street sometimes serve a delicious local speciality, curried conch served with okra. For dessert, you'll pay but a few pence for filling snack cakes and cocoa buns at the **Coronation Bakery** (★).

A typical fresh fruit and vegetable stall in Montego Bay

Boston Bay is where Jamaica's commercial jerk legend began; buy some paper-wrapped jerk from the roadside stalls (★) and settle down on the wide crescent of white sand. You will need plenty of Red Stripe beer to counteract the eye-watering sauce!

THE NORTH COAST
Almond Tree ★★★
A popularly acclaimed restaurant. Huge menu runs from hamburgers, seafood and fettucine to pepperpot, pumpkin

soup and saltfish and ackee. Dinner is served by candlelight on a terrace overlooking the sea.
Hibiscus Lodge, Main St, Ocho Rios. Tel: (876) 974 2813.

Evita's ★★★
Jamaican-Italian has found the perfect home at Evita's, where authentic pasta dishes are served on the verandah of an 1860 gingerbread house overlooking the bay. The Rasta Pasta is a must!
Eden Bower Rd, Ocho Rios. Tel: (876) 974 2333.

Jamaican cuisine

Spice is the life of Jamaican cooking. Allspice constitutes the backbone. Its source is pimento, an indigenous berry that combines the flavours of cinnamon, clove and nutmeg. Allspice was a favourite ingredient of the Arawak Indians, and Jamaica's contemporary cuisine owes much to the techniques of the early culture, combined with flavoursome Spanish and African highlights. To this exotic palette were added English and Indian influences and the spices they favoured: ginger, black pepper, cinnamon and nutmeg.

One of the most famous uses of pimento is as jerked pork, Jamaica's delicious own finger-lickin' barbecue. The meat is marinated in an incendiary mixture of island-grown spices, then cooked to mouthwatering perfection over a smoking fire of pimento wood in a scrubbed-out oil drum. It is served

Just some of the variety of good things to eat in Jamaica

straight from the coals, wrapped in paper. The Maroons perfected this cooking technique. Pepperpot soup, too, can pack a wallop. This old Taino recipe is based on callaloo, a sort of spinach, with okra, salt beef, pig tail or ham hock, and coconut meat, shallots, vegetables and the inevitable spices thrown in for good measure. If the gumbo-like broth is not hot enough, try adding some pickapeppa sauce, made from mangoes, onions, pepper, raisins, tamarinds and tomatoes.

Other zesty island dishes include curried lobster, curried goat, peppered shrimp (a delicacy of the Black River area), fresh oysters blended with vinegar and pepper, Solomon Grundy (pickled herring or mackerel), and escoveitch marinated fish fried in red pepper, onions and vinegar.

Jamaican cuisine bears a colourful lexicon. Dip-'n'-fall-back is a salty stew made of bananas and dumplings. Stamp-'n'-go is a fried, salted codfish fritter. Run-down is mackerel spiced and cooked in coconut milk, served as a breakfast dish.

Jamaica's vegetables are mostly humble. To feed the slaves cheaply, breadfruit was brought from the South Seas. From Africa came yams and ackee, whose starchy, yellow-lobed fruit (poisonous when unripe) is cooked to release its toxins, then eaten roasted, boiled or fried. Ackee looks and tastes rather like scrambled eggs. Served with onions and salted codfish, it makes the popular breakfast dish from the Harry Belafonte song, 'ackee, rice, salt fish is nice'.

Green bananas are also boiled and served as a vegetable. Cho-cho (a squashlike vegetable also known as christophine) and pumpkin are other steadfast staples, served on the side, boiled and mashed with butter.

Jamaicans rarely end a meal without fruit or a uniquely named island dessert such as 'matrimony', a marriage of green or purple star apples with pulped oranges and grapefruit in condensed milk.

A table with a view

Mr Humphrey's Pizza Café ★

Tasty pizzas, sandwiches and stuffed pittas.
Main St, Ocho Rios.
Tel: (876) 974 8319.

Ocho Rios Village Jerk Centre ★

The best jerk in town, this large outdoors place has long been popular with locals and tour groups.
Da Costa Drive, Ocho Rios. Tel: (876) 974 2549.

Ruins at the Falls ★★★

Built around an old sugar factory with seating around a Bali Hai-like lagoon facing a spectacular waterfall. Cuisine combines Jamaican with Oriental.
Da Costa Drive, Ocho Rios.
Tel: (876) 974 8888.

Toscanini ★★★★

The best restaurant in the area, set in pretty art gallery Harmony Hall. The menu is Italian with classic cooking, excellent service and a good wine list.
Harmony Hall, Tower Isle, Ocho Rios.
Tel: (876) 975 4785.

White River Ranch ★★

Cheap and cheerful jerk joint by the White River. Good Jamaican cooking, popular with locals, and late-night at the weekends.
White River, Ocho Rios.

THE WEST

In addition to the restaurants listed below, jerk barbecues come out at night and serve up delicious jerk chicken with sourdough bread. They tend to congregate outside Margaritaville in Montego Bay and along Norman Manley Boulevard in Negril.

Chicken Lavish ★

Local Jamaican cooking comes no better. Curried goat, lobster and red snapper specialities, plus mouthwatering spiced chicken.
West End Road, Negril.
Tel: (876) 957 4410.

Cosmos ★★

A popular spot serving genuine Jamaican favourites.
Norman Manley Blvd.
Tel: (876) 957 4330.

Day-O Plantation ★★★★

Lovely setting by the poolside of a plantation house. Upmarket menu with international cuisine and well-cooked Jamaican dishes such as grilled snapper and curried conch.
Fairfield, Montego Bay.
Tel: (876) 952 1825.

Evelyns ★

Long-standing restaurant in fishing community right on the water. Fish dishes of all kinds served with rice, bammy or roti bread.
Kent Ave, Whitehouse.

Houseboat Grill ★★★★

Unique location on a restored houseboat with an intriguing history now moored in Bogue Lagoon. Food is as exciting as the location, with twists on classic dishes and delicious, indulgent puddings.
Freeport Rd.
Tel: (876) 979 8845.

Pork Pit ★

Jamaican to the bone! Delicious jerk chicken and pork, with festival, sweet potatoes and yams, are eaten alfresco beneath a spreading tree.
27 Gloucester Ave, Montego Bay.
Tel: (876) 940 3008.

Rockhouse ★★★

One of Jamaica's best restaurants, with a very romantic setting right

over the sea. Blackened mahi-mahi and a seafood salad served in a coconut shell are among favourite dishes.
West End Rd, Negril.
Tel: (876) 957 4373.

Scotchies ★
Venerable jerk restaurant with a choice of chicken, pork, seafood and fish served with yams, breadfruit or festival. Tables are roadside.
Ironshore, Montego Bay.
Tel: (876) 953 3301.

Sweet Spice ★★
Local family café with modest interior and tasty Jamaican dishes. Home-made curries are particularly good.
Sheffield Rd, Negril.
Tel: (876) 957 4621.

Selina's ★★
All-day breakfast café at the back of the beach with delicious banana pancakes, fruit salads and Blue Mountain coffee roasted on site.
Norman Manley Blvd, Negril.
Tel: (876) 957 9519.

Three Dives ★
Popular and excellent jerk place with a nightly bonfire on the cliff top. Famed for its jerk lobster

and rightly so!
West End Rd, Negril.
Tel: (876) 957 0845.

Town House by the Sea ★★★★
A new location for the long-established restaurant. The menu is classy, with a dinner menu of well-prepared international cuisine – shrimp cocktail, filet mignon. Lunch is more relaxed, with sandwiches, salads and a daily special.
Gloucester Ave, Montego Bay.
Tel: (876) 952 2660.

THE SOUTH COAST
A&J Heart of Love ★★
A friendly and relaxed spot for good breakfasts and lunch. French toast, omelette and delicious salads are served alongside freshly baked bread.
Frenchman's Bay, Treasure Beach.

Bloomfield Great House ★★★★
One of Jamaica's best purveyors of 'nouvelle Jamaican' cuisine. Tables are on a terrace of a restored Great House with a revolving art exhibition on the walls.

There's an interesting wine list.
8 Perth Rd. Mandeville.
Tel: (876) 962 7130.

Culloden Café ★★
Modern Jamaican cuisine at very affordable prices. The tables are in an attractive seafront garden; the bar inside is very chic and there's a good wine selection.
Whitehouse.
Tel: (876) 963 5344.

Hotel Villa Bella ★★★
An eclectic menu of well-prepared international dishes utilises home-grown produce, including home-made ginger beer. The restaurant is in one of Jamaica's most delightful small hotels.
Christiana.
Tel: (876) 964 2243.

Jack Sprat ★★
Part of Jake's Hotel, Jack Sprat is an informal beachside café decked out like a traditional rum shop – complete with vintage jukebox. Fish and shellfish are specialities, as is home-made pizza.
Calabash Bay, Treasure Beach.
Tel: (876) 965 3583.

Rum

Rum is synonymous with Jamaica, the first Caribbean island to produce the liquor commercially. Few dispute that Jamaican rum is the best in the world.

Traditional Jamaican rums – the 'Bordeaux of the Caribbean' – are dark and full-flavoured. However, there are as many grades of rum as ways of enjoying it. Jamaican rums range from rich, aromatic dark rums to Jamaica's famous 'overproof' white rums, the strongest of all. Jamaica's 151-proof variety is fondly described as 'Jamaica's favourite poison'.

White rum is mostly the drink of the local Jamaican. The common man drinks it neat, chased down with water or coconut milk, accompanied in bars by the loud 'bang' of dominoes. Kulu kulu, the 'whitest' of white rums, has seeped into folk medicine and religious ceremony. Rastafarians even steep their *ganja* (marijuana) in the potent elixir.

Rum, from its earliest days, has been associated with life on the high seas. Sailors and pirates lent it fame, as portrayed by Robert Louis Stevenson in *Treasure Island* ('Yo, ho, ho and a bottle of rum!'). The English purchased rum on a large scale, much of it to serve the needs of the Royal Navy.

Rum is one of the purest of alcohols. It is distilled directly from sugar cane

One of Jamaica's best-selling rums

Sangster's was founded by a Scottish immigrant in 1974

without any need for the preliminary malting required to convert starch to sugar, as in other alcoholic beverages. Hence, rum retains more of its natural flavour than other liquors. Many distillers still use the original process developed by Spanish colonists, and age their rums in oak casks anywhere from three to twenty years. The type of cask lends its own colouration and flavour to the rum.

Those Jamaican rums that have been aged in barrels for over a decade are often so mellow that their subtle taste and delicate aromas can give the smoothest Cognac a run for its money.

No one knows where the word comes from. Some say that 'rum' is derived from the botanical name for sugar cane, *Saccharum officinarum*. Others suggest it originates from 'rumbullion', a word which English planters in the Bahamas used to describe the escapades it induced.

Just as rum is one of the oldest of drinks (the early Spanish first manufactured it by distilling the sweet liquor from molasses, the heavy residue of sugar-cane processing), rum punch is one of the oldest cocktails. It originated during the heyday of the sugar plantations, when English planters refined the recipe of 'sour, sweet, strong, and weak' (one part lime juice, two parts sugar, three parts rum, four parts water or fruit juice).

Hotels and accommodation

You have a world of choice. Jamaica has the largest selection of accommodation in the Caribbean – everything from lively beach resorts throbbing with reggae and old-style plantation resorts with starched linen and candelabras, to mountain inns so quiet that tree frogs sing you to sleep.

Jamaica has over 22,000 hotel rooms, and several thousand more are planned for the next few years. There is something for every budget. Many of its resorts are world-class – certainly among the best in the Caribbean (several hotels of the rich and famous offer some of the best bargains going). Jamaican hoteliers pioneered the popular all-inclusive concept (*see p175*), and these resorts continue to bring in the vast majority of tourists to the island. However, in contrast to these massive developments – the latest have 2,000 rooms – Jamaica also has a series of simple family-run guesthouses, small intimate hotels and restored Great Houses to stay in.

Mid-December through to mid-April is high season; consider low season, when rates are heavily discounted.

The **Jamaica Hotel and Tourist Association** (JHTA; *tel: (876) 926 3635; www.jhta.org*), can provide further information.

Budget hotels

There is a distinct lack of budget accommodation in Kingston, Ocho Rios and the beach areas of Montego Bay. Nevertheless, all resort areas have inexpensive guesthouses. Negril has many options, as does Treasure Beach on the south coast, while the cheapest guesthouses on the island are to be found in Port Antonio.

Budget accommodation – mountain chalets, family guesthouses and small hotels – is the norm off the tourist path. The Port Antonio Guesthouse Association (*tel: (876) 993 7118; www.go-jam.com*) represents some of the most appealing small hotels in the area. **Jamaica Cheaply** (*tel: (876) 802 2023; www.seejamaicacheaply.com*) has a range of budget accommodation, island-wide, on its website.

Business hotels

(*See pp178–9.*)

Camping and cabins

(*See p181.*)

Couples-only resorts

Two companies currently dominate the scene: the Sandals Resorts chain and Couples. The long-standing rivalry between Sandals and the Superclubs chain who invented the concept (but now prefers to concentrate on family resorts and its anything-goes Hedonism Resorts) has been a driving force in setting standards of quality throughout the Caribbean. It has also fostered a long list of firsts – satellite TV and king-size beds in all rooms, scuba diving and waterskiing as inclusions, and speciality gourmet restaurants, for example. Couples-only resorts offer lots of social activity, from volleyball games on the beach to toga parties, masquerade nights and cabaret shows.

Sandals has seven couples-only resorts in Montego Bay, Negril, Ocho Rios and at Whitehouse on the south coast. There are four Couples hotels – two in Negril and two in Ocho Rios.
Couples *Tel: in the US (001) 800 268 7537; in the UK (01582) 794 420; www.couples.com*
Sandals *Tel: in the US (001) 881-SANDALS; in the UK 0800 742 742; www.sandals.com/www.sandals.co.uk*

De luxe resorts

Perched atop their own secluded bays, some of the finest resort hotels in the Caribbean match opulence with white-gloved service. Most date from the 1950s, when Jamaica was one of the first Caribbean destinations to welcome (wealthy) tourists. Several have their own golf courses. Some are old-fashioned in an unfastidious sort of way.

It must be difficult to concentrate on eating with this view to look at

Hotels and accommodation

Options for enjoying the genteel lifestyle include:

Tryall Golf, Tennis and Beach Resort
16km (10 miles) west of Montego Bay. Tel: (876) 956 5660; www.tryallclub.com

Half Moon Resort
5km (3 miles) east of Montego Bay. Tel: (876) 953 2211; www.halfmoon.com

Round Hill
11km (7 miles) west of Montego Bay. Tel: (876) 956 7050; www.roundhilljamaica.com

Jamaica Inn
Ocho Rios. Tel: (876) 974 2514; www.jamaicainn.com

Trident Hotel
8km (5 miles) south of Port Antonio. Tel: (876) 993 2602; www.tridentjamaica.com

Inns of Jamaica

The Daily Gleaner newspaper, in conjunction with the Jamaica Tourist Board, lists 50 small hotels and inns on their website (*www.discoverjamaica. com/inns*). Some sit high above a photogenic paradise; others are close to the action. Montego Bay-based tour company **Sunshine Adventure Jamaica Ltd** has a 'Fly Drive Jamaica' (*tel: (876) 953 9505; www.flydrivejamaica.com*). You can combine car rental with vouchers for inns island-wide.

Island Outpost

Jamaican-born record producer Chris Blackwell, who founded Island Records, has diversified into a luxury hotel chain, **Island Outpost** (*tel: in the US/Canada 800 OUTPOST, in the UK 00 800 688 76781; www.islandoutpost.com*) which has four properties on Jamaica – and they are some of the loveliest small hotels on the island, much patronised by rock stars and supermodels, complete with funky décor and high walls which keep out the riffraff.

Far removed from the bland marble halls of the all-inclusive resorts, each hotel has its own distinct character. The list comprises: **The Caves**, Negril; **Jake's**, Treasure Beach; **Goldeneye**, Oracabessa; and **Strawberry Hill** in the Blue Mountains.

Spas

Jamaican holidays can easily be combined with health pursuits. Larger up-market resorts feature swimming pools, Jacuzzis, exercise rooms and, occasionally, a cold plunge, steam and sauna. Most, too, feature exercise and health classes and massage. The most comprehensive is **Couples Swept Away** (*tel: (876) 957 4061*) in Negril, which has a 4ha (10-acre) sports complex and health-spa facilities.

Spas are big business on Jamaica these days and new ones spring up every month. The best luxury spas are at the **Half Moon**, **Jamaica Inn** and **Round Hill** hotels. Most of them offer a range of treatments, using natural and locally sourced products – pineapple, coffee and aloe vera among them – and have breezy treatment rooms overlooking the sea. **The Rockhouse**

Hotel in Negril (*tel: (876) 957 0557; www.rockhouse.com*) also has a new, attractive spa on its cliff-side property.

Three-, four- or week-long packages are available with all meals and a range of treatments included through **Tiverton House** (*tel: in the US 1 (603) 4364 4721; www.jamaicaescapes.com*), a tour operator which books luxury villas on the south coast.

Oasis Spa (*tel: (876) 953 2204*), tucked away in the sleepy town of Bluefields on the south coast, is a haven of luxury treatments, scrubs, facials, wraps and massages.

The **Milk River Mineral Bath Hotel** (*tel: (876) 902 4657*) and **Bath Fountain Hotel** (*tel: (876) 703 4345*) are a little old-fashioned and cater for a mostly local clientele.

Villas

More than 40 per cent of Jamaica's accommodation is self-catering. Villas are popular island-wide and range from the quaint and cosy to the palatial, from the mountain enclave to the beachside gem. Villas are generally staffed with a housekeeper (who can double as a nanny), cook and often a gardener. Some villa owners have agreements with resorts that allow guests to use resort facilities. Several of Jamaica's finest resorts also offer villa rentals on site. For a listing of villas, apartments, condominiums and cottages, contact the **Jamaica Association of Villas and Apartments** (JAVA), PO Box 298, Ocho Rios (*tel: (876) 974 2508; in the USA call (800) 845 5276; also visit www.villasinjamaica.com*), which has an extensive list of villas on its website and can arrange package holidays including villa rental and flights.

Jaw-dropping options include **Prospect Plantation Villas** (*tel: (876) 994 1373; www.prospect-villas.com*) in Ocho Rios, **Good Hope Great House** (*tel: (876) 469 3443; www.goodhopejamaica.com*) near Falmouth and **Bluefields Villas** (*tel in the US: (001) 202 232 4010; www.bluefieldsvillas.com*).

Even more luxurious are villas at the **Tryall Club** (*tel: (876) 956 5660; www.tryallclub.com*) and **Round Hill** (*tel: (876) 956 7050; www.roundhilljamaica.com*).

Meanwhile, both **Carolyn's Caribbean Cottages** (*tel: (876) 382 6384; www.carolynscaribbeancottages. com*) and **Tiverton House** (*tel: in the US (001) 603 4364 4721; www.jamaicaescapes.com*) have a range of more unusual and quirky villas and cottages to rent.

Self-catering at Trident Villas, Port Antonio

On business

Jamaica has a thriving business community centred on Kingston, the commercial capital. The island also plays host to conventions and meetings lured by balmy weather, superb facilities and a panoply of post-business activities.

Jamaica's economic development agency, **Jamaica Promotions Corporation**, acts as the coordinating agency for business ventures between local and overseas private companies. JAMPRO promotes investment and assists investors. For information contact: *JAMPRO, Jamaica Promotions Corporation, 18 Trafalgar Rd, Kingston 5 (tel: (876) 978 7755; www.investjamaica.com).*

Similarly, the **Jamaica Chamber of Commerce** (*7 East Parade, Kingston; tel: (876) 922 0150; www.fantasyisle. com*) promotes, fosters and protects commerce and industry.

Most business offices and factories open Monday to Friday, 9am–5pm. Very few offices open on Saturday.

Business etiquette

Jamaicans do not stand on ceremony or formality. Hence, you may find your Jamaican business partner prefers casual (but usually chic) clothing.

Conference and exhibition facilities

Almost all of the larger all-inclusive resorts have sophisticated business and conference facilities, and many now have wireless internet access.

KINGSTON

The **Jamaica Conference Centre**, opened in 1973, is conveniently located in the heart of Kingston's commercial district. It was built to UN specifications and features five meeting rooms, the largest of which seats 1,050, and has 223sq m (2,400sq ft) of exhibition space. For information contact the Jamaica Conference Centre (*tel: (876) 922 9160; www.jamaicaconference.com*).

The **Courtleigh Hotel** (*85 Knutsford Blvd, Kingston 5; tel: (876) 929 9000; www.courtleigh.com*) has meeting rooms and a business centre. The **Hilton Kingston Jamaica** (*tel: (876) 926 5430; www.hilton.com*) offers full facilities for business and conferences.

The **Jamaica Pegasus Hotel** (*tel: (876) 926 3690; www.jamaicapegasus.com*) has convention facilities for up to 1,000 delegates. Nearby, the **Altamonte Grande** (*tel: (876) 929 4497; www.altamontcourt.com*) in a quieter part of new Kingston, and **Knutsford Court** (*tel: (876) 929 1000; www.knutsfordcourt.com*), both have executive conference facilities.

OCHO RIOS

Sandals Grande Ocho Rios Beach and **Villa Resort** (*tel: (876) 974 5691; www.sandals.com*) has a beach, convention and full resort facilities. The spectacular 730-room **Jamaica Grande Sunset Resort** (*tel: (876) 974 2200; www.sunsetjamaicagrande.com*) is Jamaica's largest convention hotel; it can accommodate up to 2,700 people.

MONTEGO BAY

Both the beachfront **Half Moon** resort (*tel: (876) 953 2211; www.halfmoon.com*) and the **Ritz-Carlton** (*tel: (876) 953 2204; www.ritzcarlton.com*) have excellent conference facilities.

Courier services

The postal service in Jamaica is very slow. All the big international courier services are represented in Jamaica, including **DHL** (*tel: toll-free 1-888/225 5345; www.dhl.com*) and **FedEx** (*tel: toll-free 1-888/463 3339; www.fedex.com*). Within Jamaica, both **Tara Couriers** (*tel: toll-free 1-888/827 22260; www.taracan.com*) and **Airpak Express** (*tel: (876) 663 2477; www.airpakexpress.com*) will get packages across the island within a day.

Exhibitions

An annual trade exhibition – **EXPO** – is sponsored each spring in the National Arena, Kingston, by the Jamaica Manufacturers Association (JMA; *tel: (876) 922 8880; www.jma.com.jm*) and the Jamaica Exporters Association (JEA; *tel: (876) 927 6238; www.exportjamaica.org*). **JAPEX**, Jamaica's annual travel trade exhibition, is held each April at the Sunset Jamaica Grande, Ocho Rios. Contact: The Jamaica Hotel and Tourist Association (*tel: (876) 126 3635; www.jhta.org*).

Secretarial services

The Jamaica Tourist Board can help facilitate secretarial services and equipment, as can many of the larger hotels.

The following Kingston-based companies provide secretarial and ancillary services: **Placement and Business Services Ltd** (*tel: (876) 926 8359*); and **Temps Ltd** (*tel: (876) 922 0580*). See the *Yellow Pages* for additional sources.

Translation services

English is the national tongue as well as the language of commerce. **Vilcomm International Services** (*tel: (876) 978 9399*) can provide translating and interpreting conference services.

Practical guide

Arriving

By air

Most tourists arrive by air at Donald Sangster International Airport, 3.2km (2 miles) east of Montego Bay town centre; others arrive at Norman Manley International Airport, 21km (13 miles) by road south of Kingston city centre. In either case, you face a long walk from your plane to the immigration hall.

Brace yourself for the sea of people that mills outside. There will be no shortage of hustlers waiting to hurry you into a taxi or private shuttle bus. Major resorts provide a shuttle service for pre-booked guests. Visitors on organised package tours will be met on arrival. Car rental agencies have booths outside the arrival hall, as does the Jamaica Tourist Board. **The Jamaica Union of Travellers Assocation** (JUTA; *www.jutatoursjamaica.com*) has representatives at the airport and cruise ports, and can arrange ground transfers upon arrival.

A direct (non-stop) scheduled service is available to Jamaica from Britain and other points in Europe and from several North American gateways, as well as Canada. Charter operators offer additional direct services. Scheduled flights are also available from a variety of South American countries and other islands in the Caribbean. The leading carrier is the national airline, Air Jamaica (*www.airjamaica.com*) which has the most extensive timetable.

British Airways (*www.ba.com*) and Virgin Atlantic (*www.virgin-atlantic.com*) both fly regularly from the UK. American Airlines (*www.aa.com*) and Air Canada (*www.aircanada.com*) have scheduled flights from the Americas.

There is a departure tax of J$1,000, payable in Jamaican currency or US dollars, but the vast majority of airlines include this in the price of the ticket. Check with your travel agent that this is the case.

By boat

Jamaica is a popular stopover on itineraries of several cruise companies and in 2006 won 'World's Leading Cruise Destination' at the World Travel Awards. Currently half of Jamaica's annual two million visitors come via cruise ship.

Immigration

All foreign citizens require a passport and a return or onward ticket. US, Canadian, UK and Australasian citizens are allowed to stay for six months and no visa is required (residents of other countries are allowed 90 or 30 days; stays longer than this will require a visa). An application to extend your stay must be made to the Ministry of National Security (*Mutual Life Building, North Tower, 2 Oxford Rd, Kingston 10; tel (876) 906 4908; www.mns.gov.jm*).

Camping

There are few established campsites
in Jamaica and camping rough is
not recommended. Your best bet for
camping is the gardens of small
guesthouses in Treasure Beach and
Portland who may accept tents for a
small nightly fee. **Roots Bamboo** (*tel:
(876) 957 4479; www.rootsbamboo.com*)
on the beach in Negril has a campsite,
and other places along the beach will
take campers. Other campsites include
the **Abeokuta Private Nature Park** (*tel:
(876) 823 1587*) near Bluefields, a lovely
garden with grassy lawns and a pool,
and **River Edge** (*tel: (876) 944 2673*) in
St Maria, which is a recreation park
much loved by Jamaican families.

The Blue Mountains have several
sites for hikers and campers. The best
known is Hollywell Recreational Park
which has a well-organised ranger
station which supervises the campsite.
Contact the Jamaica Conservation and
Development Trust (JCDT; *tel: (876)
960 2848; www.greenjamaica.org.jm*) in
advance to book a place.

Children

Jamaicans love children and the
country is generally safe. Great care
should be taken to prevent sunburn
and insect bites by carrying a good
supply of sunblock and insect repellent.
Use caution at waterfalls and where
coral is present. Kingston has the
Bustamante Hospital for Children
(*tel: (876) 926 5721*).
(*See also pp154–5.*)

Climate

Jamaica is a tropical island with
consistently hot, humid weather all year
round. On the north coast constant
breezes mollify the heat and humidity
so that the climate feels balmy. The
average annual temperature on the
coast is 28°C (82°F); temperatures vary
between 27 and 32°C (81 and 90°F).
Temperatures in the highlands average
5 or 6 degrees Celsius (9° or 11°F)
lower and are positively salubrious, like
an eternal spring. The Blue Mountains,
however, are much cooler. The south
coast is generally hot and moderately
dry, even semi-arid in parts.

Rainfall averages 198cm (78in) per
year, with marked regional variation.
Tropical showers can occur year-round,
most often at night. The bulk of the

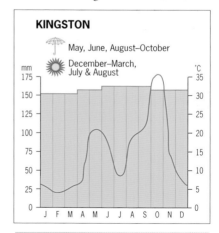

KINGSTON

May, June, August–October

December–March,
July & August

**WEATHER CONVERSION
CHART**

25.4mm = 1 inch
°F = 1.8 × °C + 32

rain falls from May to June and from September to November. The northeast coast receives three times more rain than the rest of the island.

Conversion charts
See opposite.

Crime
Jamaica is a poor country and some islanders feel forced to make a living 'scuffling' as petty thieves. Handguns are in wide circulation, and there are occasional reports of tourists being mugged on the street or robbed at gun-point in their hotel rooms. Such incidents occur relatively infrequently, although crime has shown a marked upturn in Jamaica in recent years.

Use common-sense caution. Do not carry valuables or jewellery, and carry only as much money as you need – keep the rest locked in a hotel safe. Do not leave items on view in a vehicle, on the beach or display them in public transport. Always lock car doors.

Verify the identity of anyone who calls unexpectedly at your hotel room before opening the door. (*Also see p22.*)

Parts of Kingston are sometimes subject to curfew. Avoid ghetto areas at all times. Use only licensed taxis. The British High Commission has an emergency 24-hour line (*tel: (876) 371 0496*) for British citizens only.

Customs regulations
Jamaica's incoming duty-free allowance is 25 cigars, 200 cigarettes, $^1/_2$ litre (1 pint) of liquor (except rum), 450g (1lb) of tobacco and 1 litre (2 pints) of wine. All fresh flowers, plants, honey, fruits, meats and vegetables (except canned) are restricted.

US Customs allows US$850 worth of goods after a 48-hour visit. Personal allowances for visitors 21 years or older include 200 cigarettes, 100 cigars (Cuban cigars are illegal), plus one litre of wine or spirits. Many Jamaican-made products are exempted from duty, regardless of value.

UK citizens are allowed 200 cigarettes or 50 cigars; 2 litres (3½ pints) of wine; 1 litre (1¼ pints) of spirits; 60cc/ml (2fl oz) of perfume; plus £145 of gifts, souvenirs or other goods. Remember that importation of illegal drugs or animal or plant products is subject to severe penalties.

Driving
To drive in Jamaica you need a foreign driver's licence. This is valid for up to three months; international Driver's Permits are not needed.

In general, Jamaicans drive fast, often recklessly fast considering local conditions. Watch for overtaking vehicles. The **speed limit** is 48kph (30mph) in towns and villages; 80kph (50mph) on main highways. Petrol stations are located throughout the island. **Fuel** is sold by both the litre and the gallon. Not all service stations accept credit cards or open on Sundays.

All the major international companies (Avis, Budget, Dollar, Hertz,

National) operate in Jamaica. Rental car agencies have desks in major hotels and at Montego Bay and Kingston airports. Car hire charges can give you a shock – Jamaica is one of the most expensive places in the Caribbean. Largest and among the least expensive is **Island Car Rentals** (*tel: (876) 926 8861; www.islandcarrentals.com*), with offices throughout Jamaica. Other companies are listed in the *Yellow Pages.*

Cars with a driver can be hired from the **Jamaica Union of Travellers Association** (JUTA).

Motor scooters and motorcycles can be rented from roadside offices in all the major resorts.

Car rental fees cover driver's **insurance**. Collision Damage Waiver insurance is offered by rental agencies; without it you will be assessed for damage from a minimum of $500. Before leaving home, check to see whether your existing car insurance covers you. Some credit cards also provide coverage for international car rental. Carefully scrutinise the car before accepting it for pre-existing damage (including dents and scratches) and to see that items shown on the checklist are actually functioning.

If involved in an **accident**, do not move, or let anyone else move, the vehicles. Don't allow yourself to get drawn into an argument. Have someone else call the police. Remain at the scene until a police officer arrives. If you have a camera, take a photo of the scene. Obtain the name and address of

Practical guide

CONVERSION TABLE

FROM	TO	MULTIPLY BY
Inches	Centimetres	2.54
Feet	Metres	0.3048
Yards	Metres	0.9144
Miles	Kilometres	1.6090
Acres	Hectares	0.4047
Gallons	Litres	4.5460
Ounces	Grams	28.35
Pounds	Grams	453.6
Pounds	Kilograms	0.4536
Tons	Tonnes	1.0160

To convert back, for example from centimetres to inches, divide by the number in the third column.

MEN'S SUITS

UK	36	38	40	42	44	46	48
Rest of Europe	46	48	50	52	54	56	58
USA	36	38	40	42	44	46	48

DRESS SIZES

UK	8	10	12	14	16	18
France	36	38	40	42	44	46
Italy	38	40	42	44	46	48
Rest of Europe	34	36	38	40	42	44
USA	6	8	10	12	14	16

MEN'S SHIRTS

UK	14	14.5	15	15.5	16	16.5	17
Rest of Europe	36	37	38	39/40	41	42	43
USA	14	14.5	15	15.5	16	16.5	17

MEN'S SHOES

UK	7	7.5	8.5	9.5	10.5	11
Rest of Europe	41	42	43	44	45	46
USA	8	8.5	9.5	10.5	11.5	12

WOMEN'S SHOES

UK	4.5	5	5.5	6	6.5	7
Rest of Europe	38	38	39	39	40	41
USA	6	6.5	7	7.5	8	8.5

those involved in the accident as well as the make and licence number of other vehicles. Record the names and addresses of any witnesses. Make sure you inform your rental company as soon as possible.

Car hire companies provide an emergency telephone number to call in the event of a **breakdown**. Most have 24-hour emergency service. Off the beaten track, locals will offer their services as mechanics; use your discretion. The *Yellow Pages* lists automobile repair services.

Electricity
The standard electricity supply is 110 volts/50 cycles; 220 volts is available in some hotels. Large hotels can supply adaptors as needed. Many rural homes have electricity.

Embassies and consulates
British High Commission
28 Trafalgar St, Kingston.
Tel: (876) 510 0700/emergency 24 hour line (876) 371 0496; www. britishhighcommission.gov.uk/Jamaica
Canadian High Commission
www.cic.gc.ca
French Embassy
13 Hillcrest Ave, Kingston 6.
Tel: (876) 978 0210.
German Embassy
www.konsulate.de/jamaica
US Embassy
142 Old Hope Rd, Kingston 6.
Tel: (876) 702 6000.
kingston.usembassy.gov

Emergency numbers
Air-Sea Rescue 119; **Ambulance** 110; **Fire** 110; **Police** 119.

Health
No vaccinations are required to enter Jamaica. Standards of health are generally high. All tap water in Jamaica is purified and filtered. It is wise to wash all fruit and vegetables.

Sunburn is a potential problem. Do not underestimate the strength of the tropical sun. It's always best to use sunblocks.

Most large hotels have a resident nurse. There are public and private hospitals in all major towns – all have 24-hour emergency facilities. Smaller towns have health clinics and doctors' offices (see *Yellow Pages* under 'Physicians' for listings). Check your personal insurance before leaving home to avoid additional expensive premiums in Jamaica.
Falmouth Falmouth Hospital.
Tel: (876) 954 3250.
Kingston Public Hospital.
Tel: (876) 922 0210.
Mandeville Mandeville Hospital.
Tel: (876) 625 8493.
Montego Bay Cornwall Regional Hospital. *Tel: (876) 952 5100.*
Ocho Rios St Ann's Bay Hospital.
Tel: (876) 927 2272.
Port Antonio Port Antonio General Hospital. *Tel: (876) 993 2646.*
University Hospital at Mona
Tel: (876) 927 1620.

Hitch-hiking

Hitch-hiking is a way of life for Jamaicans. Schoolchildren, for example, typically hitch between school and home. If driving, you will be waved down for a ride all along your route. If hitching, stretch your arm out and wave your hand up and down to attract a ride.

Insurance

Travel insurance to cover unforeseen medical expenses and loss of property is highly recommended. Consider purchasing cancellation insurance to protect against the cost of unused travel services in the event that you must cancel your trip. Driver's insurance is included in the cost of car hire (*see pp183–4*).

Internet

Many of the big resorts now have a wireless internet business centre with internet facilities. Several of the smaller hotels will allow you to plug your own laptop into the telephone dataport. Cyber cafés abound, especially in the larger tourist areas.

Marriage

Tying the knot is a civil ceremony. You must have been on the island for 24 hours and possess a birth certificate (those under 21 need a letter of parental consent), and divorce or death certificates if divorced or widowed.

Hotels can make all the arrangements. Most require you to send notarised copies and photocopies of passports six weeks in advance. Tour operators usually provide full details of necessary documentation and a package is the cheaper and easier way to arrange an island wedding. Otherwise, apply to the Ministry of Social Security and Labour (*1F North St, Kingston; tel: (876) 922 9500; www.mlss.gov.jm*) or contact the JTB (*www.visitjamaica.com*) worldwide for assistance.

For a religious ceremony, contact clergymen in advance.

Measurements *See p183.*

Media

Leading newspapers include the *Daily Gleaner* (*www.jamaica-gleaner.com*) and the *Observer* (*www. jamaicaobserver. com*) morning dailies and *The Star* (*www.jamaica-star.com*), an afternoon tabloid. *Jamaica Tourist* (*www.jamaicatourist.net*) is a free newspaper issued in March, July and November with features and listings.

There are half a dozen listenable radio stations. **RJR** (*www.rjr94fm.com*) is the most traditional, with talk and sport, while the most popular, heard everywhere all over the island, is music station **Irie FM** (*www.iriefm.net*). **Power 106** (*www.go-jamaica.com/ power*) has a range of excellent, opinionated talk shows.

The BBC World Service is broadcast, as is **BBC Caribbean** (*www. bbc.co.uk/ caribbean*), which is a good source of local and international news.

There are two television stations, **TVJ** and **CVM Television**. Local newspapers publish TV guides. North American cable channels are available in most larger hotels.

Money

Bank hours are Monday to Thursday 9am–2pm and Friday 9am–3pm or 4pm. Official currency is the Jamaica dollar (J$), divided into 100 cents. Notes are issued in denominations of J$50, J$100, J$500 and J$1000. Coins are J$1, J$5, J$10 and J$20.

There is no limit to the amount of foreign currency you may bring in. It is illegal to change foreign currency except at banks, hotels and other authorised dealers. A commission is charged for converting currency.

US dollars are widely accepted when paying for hotels, car rentals, duty-free shopping and meals in tourist resorts. ATMs in the larger resorts dish out US dollars as well as Jamaican currency; look out for Cool Cash outlets. Travellers' cheques can be changed in banks and those in US dollar denominations can also be used for some purchases. Major credit cards are accepted in hotels and many restaurants and stores in major towns such as Kingston, Montego Bay, Negril and Ocho Rios. It is advisable to keep some Jamaican currency for use in local stores and markets and for buying food from street vendors. Sales Tax (GCT) is 16.5 per cent.

National holidays

1 January New Year's Day
Variable Ash Wednesday
Variable Good Friday
Variable Easter Monday
23 May Labour Day
1st Monday in August Independence Day
3rd Monday in October National Heroes Day
25 December Christmas Day
26 December Boxing Day

Opening hours

Offices and factories open Monday to Friday 9am–5pm. Stores generally open Monday to Saturday 8.30am–5pm. Some stores in tourist resorts stay open seven days a week, including early evening.

Organised tours

Dozens of local tour companies offer day- and multi-day excursions. For sightseeing services, enquire at hotel desks or with the Jamaica Tourist Board. Recommended standard tour operators with proven track records are: Caribic Vacations (*tel: (876) 953 9895; www.caribicvacations.com*); Glamour Transport and Tours Ltd (*tel: (876) 940 3277; www.glamourtoursdmc.com*); Tourwise (*tel: (876) 974 2323; www.tourwisejamaica.com*); Tropical Tours Ltd (*tel: (876) 953 9100; www.tropicaltours-ja.com*).

Pharmacies

All standard medicines and toiletries are available. Hours of opening vary widely. Each major town and resort has at least one late-night and/or Sunday-opening pharmacy.

Police

The police speak English and are generally helpful. Montego Bay, Negril and Ocho Rios have special tourism liaison officers. Main resort areas have special uniformed tourism assistants.

Post offices

Every town has a post office. The reception desks at most hotels sell postage stamps and will accept letters and postcards for mailing. Some will also handle packages (charges can be added to your bill). Allow a minimum one week for delivery to Europe or North America.
Standard opening hours are Mon–Fri 9am–5pm.

Public transport

Public transportation is not one of Jamaica's strong points. Local **bus services** connect all villages and towns. though this method of transport is not generally recommended. The service is disorganised, buses are overcrowded, and schedules are flexible. One exception is the new Knutsford Express (*tel: (876) 462 2822*) which runs an air-conditioned coach between the Montego Bay bus park and New Kingston twice daily. Fares are less than

A friendly police officer

US$25 one-way and include newspapers and bottled water.

Minibuses are the cheapest, and most crowded, way to get around (J$2–J$5 virtually anywhere). Outside towns they can be flagged down. Contact the Tourist Board for departure points.

Taxis (called contract carriages) are widely available. In Kingston, some taxis are metered, but not elsewhere. Negotiate a price before you get in (consult your hotel concierge beforehand for appropriate rates). Taxis have prescribed charges between given points, but few drivers adhere to this. Licensed taxis display red PPV plates (Public Passenger Vehicle); other taxis are unlicensed and should be avoided as they can be unsafe.

The Jamaica Union of Travellers Association (JUTA; *www.*

jutatoursjamaica.com) operates special tourist taxis and buses, including ground transfers. Prices are controlled. Contact the following offices for rates and reservations:

Falmouth *Tel: (876) 954 2684.*
Kingston *Tel: (876) 927 4534.*
Montego Bay *Tel: (876) 952 0813.*
Negril *Tel: (876) 952 9197.*
Ocho Rios *Tel: (876) 974 2292.*
Port Antonio *Tel: (876) 993 2684.*

The domestic airline Air Jamaica (*tel: (876) 922 3460; www.airjamaica.com*) runs a frequent shuttle service between Montego Bay and Kingston. Charter service International Air Link (*tel: (876) 940 6660; www.intlairlink.com*) operates regular flights to Negril and Ocho Rios and can also be chartered to Port Antonio.

Senior citizens

Few concessions are offered for senior citizens. Seniors' travel clubs in your home country may offer special tour packages.

Sustainable tourism

Thomas Cook is a strong advocate of ethical and fairly traded tourism and believes that the travel experience should be as good for the places visited as it is for the people who visit them. That's why we firmly support The Travel Foundation, a charity that develops solutions to help improve and protect holiday destinations, their environment, traditions and culture. To find out what you can

do to make a positive difference to the places you travel to and the people who live there, please visit *www.thetravelfoundation.org.uk*

Telephones

Direct international telephone service operates 24 hours a day. Most up-market hotels have a direct-dial service, though charges are often excessive.

Jamaica has been revolutionised by the arrival of mobile phones and Jamaicans are now said to have more mobiles per household than any other nation. The long-standing monopoly by Cable and Wireless (*tel: (876) 926 9700; www.home.cwjamaica.com*) the national telecommunications network, was broken several years ago by Irish company Digicel (*tel: (876) 960 2696; www.digiceljamaica.com*) who offered a cheap mobile phone service to all.

If you have a tri-band phone, the easiest – and cheapest – way to make phone calls is to buy a Digicel pre-paid SIM card from any one of numerous outlets islandwide. This is then topped up by buying Flex cards or credit from supermarkets, service stations and many other locations.

Big resorts and hotels in Jamaica rent phones to guests for a small fee, as do both Cable and Wireless and Digicell. Otherwise, try Cellular Abroad (*www.cellularabroad.com*).

AT&T USA Direct Service to the USA is available from select hotels and telephone offices island-wide. From hotels call *872*; or for reverse charge (collect) calls from other phones, dial *1*. The operator can place your call and bill your AT&T account.

For operator assistance call *112* (domestic) or *113* (international). For directory assistance call *114*.

A good calling card is the local pre-paid World Talk, widely available all over Jamaica.

Coin-operated public telephones are widely available, and instructions are posted. If using a calling card do not give the number to anyone but a telephone operator. Service is irregular, reception sometimes erratic.

International Codes: Australia *61*; **Ireland** *535*; **South Africa** *27*; **United Kingdom** *44*; **USA and Canada** *1*.

Time

Jamaica is on US Eastern Standard Time; GMT less 6 hours (spring/summer); GMT less 5 hours (autumn/winter). Daylight Saving Time is not observed in Jamaica.

Tipping

Most hotels and restaurants add a 10 to 15 per cent service charge. If not, tip according to quality of service. All-inclusive resorts do not allow tipping.

Toilets

There are virtually no public facilities in Jamaica. Most large hotels have toilet facilities.

Tourist offices

The Jamaica Tourist Board promotes tourism and handles information. They can provide general information and maps, plus an information holiday guide (*www.visitjamaica.com*).

There are no longer JTB services in Negril or Ocho Rios – these are handled there by the TPDCO (The Tourist Product Development Company; *www.tpdco.org*).

Head Office 64 Knutsford Blvd, Kingston 5. *Tel: (876) 929 9200.*

Montego Bay Cornwall Beach. *Tel: (876) 952 4425.*

Ocho Rios Ocean Village Shopping Centre. *Tel: (876) 974 7705.*

Negril Times Square. *Tel: (876) 957 9314.*

Port Antonio City Centre Plaza. *Tel: (876) 993 3051.*

Offices abroad

UK 1–2 Prince Consort Rd, London SW7 2BZ. *Tel: (020) 7225 9090.*

USA 5201 Blue Lagoon Drive, Suite # 670, Miami, Fl 33126. *Tel: (305) 665 0557.*

Canada 303 Eglinton Ave East, Suite 200, Toronto, ONT M4P IL3. *Tel: (416) 482 7850.*

Travellers with disabilities

Jamaica is not well set up for travellers with disabilities. Streets and pavements are uneven and there are no ramps. Many resorts are at both beach and street level.

Some newer resort hotels take into account the needs of the disabled.

Index

Acknowledgements

Thomas Cook wishes to thank the photographers, picture libraries and other organisations for the loan of the photographs reproduced in this book, to whom copyright in the photographs belongs.

Nick Hanna/ALAMY 77
ETHEL DAVIES 8, 11, 12, 13, 16a, 19, 26, 43, 65, 72, 85, 95, 100, 126, 133, 135
FLICKR/Smikulen 62, B K Weaver 78, Edu-Tourist 79, Run With Scissors 81, en-tact 84, bhell13 86, BitHead 99, sparkyd 137, byrnesyliam 139, Trojan Warrior 152, Ostinatom 153, Jake Brewer 155, Jamdowner 162, Brian Bush 165
FOTOLIA/Marius Jasaitis 23
PICTURES COLOUR LIBRARY 24
THOMAS COOK TOUR OPERATIONS LTD 1
WORLD PICTURES/Photoshot 24, 53, 54, 71, 187

The remaining photographs are held in the AA PHOTO LIBRARY and were taken by JON WYAND, with the exception of 27, 105, 113, 117, 140, 146, 159, 161 and 168 which were taken by R VICTOR

Proofreader: JAN McCANN for CAMBRIDGE PUBLISHING MANAGEMENT LTD

SEND YOUR THOUGHTS TO
BOOKS@THOMASCOOK.COM

We're committed to providing the very best up-to-date information in our travel guides and constantly strive to make them as useful as they can be. You can help us to improve future editions by letting us have your feedback. If you've made a wonderful discovery on your travels that we don't already feature, if you'd like to inform us about recent changes to anything that we do include, or if you simply want to let us know your thoughts about this guidebook and how we can make it even better – we'd love to hear from you.

Send us ideas, discoveries and recommendations today and then look out for your valuable input in the next edition of this title.

Emails to the above address, or letters to Travellers Project Editor, Thomas Cook Publishing, PO Box 227, Coningsby Road, Peterborough PE3 8SB, UK.

Please don't forget to let us know which title your feedback refers to!